THIS BOOK IS FOR...

anyone in your company who talks to a customer.

THIS BOOK IS PRICELESS FOR...

Salespeople and their Managers
Entrepreneurs
Receptionists
The Accounting Department
Collections
Production
Shipping
Design/Engineering
The Human Resources Department
Repairs
the "Help Desk"
the "Service Department"
Every Manager
Every Corporate Officer
and the CEO

THIS BOOK CAN DETERMINE...

whether the customer's next call to you will be an order
or a cancellation.

THIS BOOK IS PURE GOLD FOR...

anyone who picks up the phone and says, "Hello."

THIS BOOK IS FOR...

You!

Satisfied customers
will shop *anywhere!*

Loyal customers will
encourage others to buy
from you, and *FIGHT*
before they switch!

Which would you
rather have --
1,000 satisfied customers,
or 1,000 *loyal*
customers?

Why America's Business Leaders Are Telling You to Buy This Book

"A book that every employee, manager, and entrepreneur in America should own, read, and put into action before their competition does."

Harvey Mackay
Author of Dig Your Well Before You're Thirsty
and Swim with the Sharks Without Being Eaten Alive

"So powerful that I read the book in one sitting! A conceptual breakthrough in understanding how customer service can grow a business."

Mark Ethridge
Publisher
Business Journal of Charlotte

"Right on the mark! No nonsense approach packed with wisdom and insights to improve all aspects of customer retention -- the key to survival of any business."

Mark Steinberg
Vice President of Sales
Wausau Insurance

"You better read this book from cover to cover before your competition does! Great common sense ideas that are easy to implement."

John Hillerich IV
President
PowerBilt Golf

"Fun reading, packed with powerful bite-sized ideas. If you want to deliver memorable service, you will find page after page of valuable information."

Dennis Tamcsin
Senior Vice President
Northwestern Mutual Life

"Forget everything you thought you knew about customer satisfaction. Jeffrey Gitomer weaves his unique style into a dramatic and exciting approach to what taking care of customers really means."

Shari L. Dilg
CSI Director
Cintas, The Uniform People

"Visionary thoughts on customer loyalty! I rate this book as highly as the *Inc.* seminars attendees rate Jeffrey's presentations -- #1."

Kevin Gilligan
Senior Conference Producer
Inc. *Magazine Seminars*

"Once I picked up the book and started to read I was hooked! Jeffrey Gitomer has written a book that outlines the principles of customer service fundamental for any successful business. I highly recommend it."

Michael J. Leone
General Manager
Radisson Hotel, Pittsburgh

"If you read Jeffrey's column every week in the *Business Journal*, you'll love having this library at your fingertips for your daily dose of great customer service ideas."

Gerald Yuille
Assistant Vice President
NationsBank

"Jeffrey's real-life examples hit home and make you realize the true difference between satisfaction and loyalty."

Dawn Josephson
Editor
Cutting Edge Media

"What a concise, powerful tool for any company and every person!"

Nido Qubein
Speaker and author of Achieving Peak Performance

"Most compelling resource I've ever read on customer service. Jeffrey changes our perception of customer satisfaction with practical and real loyalty methods that are priceless."

Julio Melara
President
Baton Rouge Business Report
Author of It Only Takes Everything You've Got

"If you're interested in climbing to the top of your industry, have every employee use this book to create a 'loyalty' action plan. Explosive results will unfold."

Brian Gendron
General Manager
Hendrick Lexus

"WOW! This is dynamite. If you want to be a successful survivor in the next century, read and study this book. These teachings apply to manufacturing, marketing, and sales."

Ted B. Owens
Senior Territory Manager
Milliken and Company

"A fresh and provocative approach to sales and marketing problems. Most sales executives don't think in these terms."

Bruce Levinson
President & CEO
Paramount Headwear, Inc.

"Simple, entertaining, and powerful! This book will be a real tool for PowerBilt Golf. It's a must read for all employees that deal with customers -- in other words, everyone."

Larry Edlin
Director of U.S. Sales
PowerBilt Golf

"Awesome! Brilliant! I wish everyone I do business with would read this book."

Richard Brodie
CEO, Brodie Technology Group, Inc.
Author of Virus of the Mind *and* Getting Past OK

THE REALITY AND VALUE OF LOYAL.
Gold *every* way you look at it.

Loyal as a dog. All have heard it and most have experienced it. What a wonderful feeling to have the unconditional love and affection that comes from loyalty. It is the highest form of friendship and the highest form of commitment.

A loyal pet.
A loyal servant.
A loyal friend.
A loyal spouse.
A loyal fan.

Loyal is unyielding, unrelenting, and ever faithful. True to the end. It is with that understanding that this book is centered.

So, how do you get to "loyal" in the relationships with your customers? Simple -- apply the principles that build loyalty in every other aspect of your life. Well, sort of simple. Loyalty is more delicate with customers because there is a balance of money and value. And loyalty is not just granted -- it's an earned distinction.

Loyalty is the highest mark.
Loyalty is success.
Loyalty is solid gold.
Loyalty is golden business.
And your golden opportunity to win by earning it from others.

But I *know* you.
You want the easiest answers, don't you?
You want the fastest answers, don't you?
You want the best answers, don't you?
You want the answers that are accepted by others, don't you?
You want the answers that are praised by others, don't you?
You want the right answers, don't you?

Well, there *are* easy answers -- but you have to work hard to achieve mastery of them. This book helps you discover those loyalty answers. *And* the best ways to master them.

Look out for the (loyalty) locomotive!

Worthless. "Can I help you?" If you were shopping in a store your reply would be, "No thanks, just looking." Then the clerk might say, "Well, just holler if you need me."

Not a very memorable exchange. But in the end you may buy something and leave the store as a satisfied customer. *Big deal*.

Will you return to the store? *Maybe*. Will you tell anyone else you were there? *Maybe*. How will that type of exchange breed loyalty? *It won't*.

Memorable. This book is about memorable, and how you can get there. Suppose you were walking into a store and an energetic, friendly young woman greets you with, "Welcome to Acme Clothing. My name is Amy (she shakes your hand and you offer your name, Bill Johnson). Mr. Johnson, most people who come in the store are just looking, but take a minute with me and let me show you what just came in -- I'm excited about it, and you'll *love* it."

See the difference? Not that difficult to do. Yet it makes a BIG difference in the perception of the customer.

Word of Mouth. Customers need service all the time in all kinds of ways. Some are happy when they call, some are so mad they can't see straight. This book is how to serve them in a way that they will go away ecstatic, tell their friends how great you were, come back again for more, ask for you personally, and bring their friends with them. WOW!

Understandable. This book is laced with examples and stories from my life as a cash-paying customer -- some are hilarious -- some will make you applaud -- some will make you nauseous -- some will even make you throw up.

Real World. I learned this stuff as a customer in hotels, on airplanes, and buying stuff in stores -- trying to spend my money -- from people who often refused to take YES for an answer.

It's getting harder to spend your money anywhere in this country without getting **pissed off** -- or at least disappointed at the level of service received.

JEFFREY GITOMER

YOUR WORLD.
Check out the bottom of each chapter --
many contain the phrase "Get Real"...

...

That's the time for you to pause and think about
how this information affects you. Puts you in the
customer's shoes.

EASY TO WIN. And in some cases you are offered a way
to start using the information immediately with a
"Just try this" idea.

...

Something you can try and get a feel for the concept.
Something to make the bridge from where you are
(satisfied) to where you need to be (loyal).

PRICELESS. Welcome to the book about loyalty and
how to build it in others and build your success at
the same time. WOW!

All Aboard THE LOYALTY EXPRESS...
a train that will train you and provide a memorable
ride for your customers. And you keep all the tickets
and end up with all the money!
What a country!

CUSTOMER
SATISFACTION
IS
WORTHLESS

JEFFREY
GITOMER

CUSTOMER
LOYALTY IS
PRICELESS

CUSTOMER SATISFACTION IS WORTHLESS

CUSTOMER LOYALTY IS PRICELESS

How to
make customers *love* you,
keep them coming back
and tell *everyone*
they know

by
JEFFREY GITOMER

BARD PRESS
AUSTIN

CUSTOMER SATISFACTION IS WORTHLESS, CUSTOMER LOYALTY IS PRICELESS
How to make customers *love* you, keep them coming back,
and tell *everyone* they know

Copyright © 1998 by Jeffrey Gitomer

Printed in the United States of America
Permission to reproduce or transmit in any form or by any means,
electronic or mechanical, including photocopying and recording,
or by an information retrieval system, must be obtained in writing
from the publisher.
Call or write Bard Press,
5275 McCormick Mtn Dr., Austin, TX 78734
Phone: 512-266-2112, Fax: 512-266-2749, E-mail: ray@bardpress.com

Visit our Web site at www.bardpress.com

ISBN: 1-885167-30-X hardcover

Library of Congress Cataloging-in-Publication Data

Gitomer, Jeffrey H.
        Customer satisfaction is worthless, customer loyalty is priceless:
    how to make customers love you, keep them coming back, and tell
    everyone they know / by Jeffrey Gitomer.
            p.   cm.
        Includes index.
        ISBN 1-885167-30-X
        1. Customer loyalty. 2. Consumer satisfaction. 3. Customer
    services. 4. Customer relations. I. Title.
    HF5415.525.G58 1998
    658.8' 12--dc21   98- 17427
                                                                          CIP
To order additional copies of this title,
contact your local bookstore or call 704.333.1112.
The author may be contacted at the following address:
Buy|Gitomer
310 Arlington Avenue, Loft 329
Charlotte, NC 28203
Phone: 512-266-2112, Fax: 512-266-2749, E-mail: ray@bardpress.com

Printings: First – May 1998; Second – November 1998;   Third – May 1999;
Fourth – March 2000;   Fifth – February 2001;   Sixth – September 2001;
Seventh – February 2002;   Eighth – June 2002;   Ninth – February 2003;
Tenth – June 2003;   Eleventh – November 2003;   Twelfth – July 2004;
Thirteenth – November 2004; Fourteenth – April 2005;   Fifteenth – December 2005

A BARD PRESS BOOK

Developmental Editor: Rod Smith
Word Processing Manager: Sherry Sprague
Proofreaders: Deborah Costenbader, Marty St. Onge
Cover Design: gary hixson
Text Design/Production: gary hixson
Index: Linda Webster

TABLE OF

CONTENTS

CONTENTS [EXPANDED LISTING]

EXPANDED contents

EXPANDED **contents**

If you listen to Corporate America blow their own horn, they'll tell you... Customer satisfaction is at an all-time high. The fact is... **Customer loyalty is at an all-time low.**

JEFFREY GITOMER

Customers, the Source of Your Paycheck

INTRODUCING THE MOST IMPORTANT PERSON IN THE WORLD

- An "important" discovery
- The fortune being made in service -- and the fortune being lost
- What's in this book for you? *Lots!*
- How do you want to be served? (*the diamond rule of service*)
- Good News!
- We will disagree once

When you're speaking with a customer, who's the most important person in the world?

"THE CUSTOMER!" you all say.

Oh really? Let's look at it a different way -- suppose there were two people left on the face of the earth -- you and your customer. One of you had to die. Who do you want to see drop dead?

"THE CUSTOMER!" you all say.

So we now have established that YOU are the most important person in the world. The problem is when you're speaking with a customer they think that THEY are the most important person in the world -- and your job is to treat them that way -- but you don't.

You say...
- The person who takes care of that is on vacation for a week.
- We're out of stock, and I don't know when we'll have more.
- I'm sorry, this is the best we can do.
- That's not my job.
- I don't care how you got it before -- this is the way we do it now.
- I don't have to take this.
- (*computer voice*) Your call will be answered in the order in which it was received.
- I'm either on my phone or away from my desk.
- Our policy says...

You hate it when it happens to you, don't you? Well, this may come as a shock, but you (or someone in your company) may be saying these very same things to your customers.

In this book, you will discover simple strategies and techniques you can put into immediate action that will make your customers feel like you want to feel when you're the customer. *Cool.*

The fortune being made in service -- and the fortune being lost.

"We have a 97.5% *customer satisfaction* rating!" Big deal.

That means 2.5% of your customers are mad and they're telling everyone. And 97.5% of your customers will shop anyplace the next time they go to market for your product or service.

Satisfied customers will shop anyplace. LOYAL customers will fight before they switch -- AND they will proactively refer people to buy from you.

That's the premise -- here's the challenge. *How do you make customers loyal?* It's easy -- you concentrate on loyalty instead of satisfaction. It's a mindset combined with an understanding of the concepts and a dedication to take actions (perform) in new ways.

The reward is a loyal customer -- the consequence is a lost customer -- or at least a wishy-washy one.

"I'M SATISFIED..."

What is a satisfied customer? One that felt OK about dealing with you. Their needs were met. The product was OK. The service was OK. The experience was OK. They are satisfied (happy) with their purchase. They may or may not talk about the experience. They may or may not refer someone to you. Their overall feeling about you is between neutral and positive, and their experiences with you have not been negative. Not bad -- but not great.

"I'M LOYAL..."

What is a loyal customer? One who feels GREAT about dealing with you. Their needs were met and/or exceeded. Your delivery was GREAT. The service was GREAT. The experience was GREAT. They are ecstatic with their purchase. They will proactively talk about the experience. They will proactively refer someone to you. Their overall feeling about you is wonderful and their experiences with you have been memorable. WOW!

What's in this book for you?
What will you take away?

Here's a dozen reasons
every person in your company should
master this book before your
competition does.

First: This book is easy!
Easy to read.
Easy to understand.
Easy to do (*and easy NOT to do*).

Second: This book is a meal!
Meat and Potatoes.
No Marshmallow Fluff.
Just facts, principles, self-evaluation tests,
ideas, action steps to success, stories you
can relate to, stories you can learn from,
stories you will enjoy, laughs,
and truths...
major truths.

Third: This book is real!

It defines customer service in terms of the
real-world actions you take every day.

It offers ANSWERS to real-world situations
that will make you a hero to your customer,
and a success for yourself.

Fourth: This book is ugly!

It defines the present situation of customer service
today...and what's wrong with it:

☞ bad, and getting worse
(The bigger the company -- the worse the service.)

☞ companies distancing themselves
from customers
(Automated attendant. Press one, press two...)

☞ companies train in terms of their "policy"
(Customers don't care about policy.)

☞ employees care about self,
not customers or company
(Companies care about self and have no loyalty to employees.)

☞ employees don't see training as
"for themselves," rather as a pain in the
butt and a "necessary evil" of the job.
*(Companies ignore personal development training
and concentrate on company training.)*

☞ service people are not prepared to serve
in a memorable way.
*(Training is based on "satisfying" the customer,
the lowest level of acceptable service.)*

Introducing the Most Important Person in the World 01

Fifth: This book is blunt!

If you hate it when you get lousy service,
why do you (your company) give
lousy service to others?

The customer could care less about you,
your company or your company policy, and even LESS
about "why you can't" give them what they want.

They want YES, or help in getting to yes,
and if you can't help them, they'll go someplace else
(*and take their money and their word-of-mouth
advertising with them*).

How do *you* want to be served?
Are you serving the same way?

☞ The Diamond Rule of Service...

If you wouldn't want it done to you, don't do it to someone else!

Sixth: This book teaches you how to be the best!

It defines the principles of developing loyalty.

IT TEACHES...

☞ how to say everything in terms of the customer.

☞ how to say yes and be friendly in every situation.

☞ how to have fun on the job.

☞ how to get customers to tell good stories about you.

☞ how to get customers to be loyal.

It converts the principles and lessons of each story or example -- and shows you how to take action. *Now!*

Seventh: This book shows you YOU!

☞ 7 self-evaluation tests that tell you how to use the results to make *you* a raging success on and off the job.

☞ the personal development lessons you never learned in school, but need to be a success in whatever you do in your career.

01

Introducing the Most Important Person in the World

Eighth: This book is pleasure/pain!

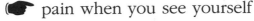 pain when you see yourself

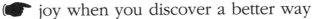 joy when you discover a better way

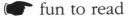 pleasure when you see the reaction
of customers

Ninth: This book is fun and funny!

 fun to read

 laced with humor

 will make you laugh out loud

Tenth: This book is answers!

 simple solutions

 easy-to-implement answers

 success formulas

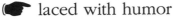 real-world examples

self-evaluations

useable lessons

actions to take *now*

Eleventh: This book challenges the way you do it today!

I say Customer Satisfaction is Worthless --

"Wait just a second there," you say.
"Customer satisfaction is important!"
I agree. It is important.

It's just that on the ladder of customer service
importance, the ladder of success,
"customer satisfaction"
is the lowest rung.

CUSTOMER LOYALTY is the top rung.

Twelfth: This book is now and tomorrow!

☞ Principles and strategies you can put into practice the minute you read them, and turn them into loyal customers, repeat business, bigger tips, memorable stories about you, and unsolicited referrals.

☞ Ways to out-serve your competition today to ensure your success tomorrow.

Introducing the Most Important Person in the World

01

Here's some good news
if your service is somewhere between
mediocre and satisfactory.

There are so few examples of memorable service
that people write books about the great incidents,
and other people buy the books
by the millions
to read about what should be
an ordinary everyday experience.

If you take the information and strategies
that this book offers, and put them into action,
you can establish a dominant leadership position
in your community,
your region,
your market,
and your industry --
just on the strength of your service.

I hope you do.

We will only disagree on one point.

The only place in this book
where we will disagree is at the end.

When you're done reading the book
you'll hope your competition
never buys this book or reads it --

and I hope they do.

The cost of

fixing the wrong,

making amends,

making it right,

creating a memorable recovery

-- and adding (*giving*)

something unexpected

to the customer (*discount, free gift*)

is ALWAYS less than the cost

of an upset (*angry*) customer

and a negative story about you

that is retold for years.

> The customer only wants two things -- show me you care about me personally, and tell me what you're going to do for me now (help me, please).
>
> JEFFREY GITOMER

INTRODUCING THE CUSTOMER (HELP!)

- These days customers are...
- HELP! Why do customers call us?
  (*What do they want?*)
- Shouldn't it really be called "Customer Helping"?
- What else would customers like?
- Define your customer
- What's one customer worth?
- The 21st century customer service challenge
- Treat them like...

These days customers are...

✔ Smarter

✔ Leaner

✔ Price conscious

✔ Lower morale (downsized)

✔ Hit on more by competitors

AND -- because of poor service expectations, these customers are also...

✔ More demanding

✔ Less forgiving

✔ Harder to satisfy

✔ Less loyal

Why do customers call us?
What do they want?

Customers call for one reason, they want...

- "Help, I need an answer!"
- "Help, I need information on my order!"
- "Help, I need service!"
- "Help, I have a question!"
- "Help, I want to place an order!"
- "Help, something's wrong or broken!"
- "Help, I need to speak to someone!"
- "Help! Help! Help!"

Do we give them help? No. What do we give them?
Well, we almost give them help...
We give them H e l ... l
They want help. We give hell.

"Our policy says..."
"She's not here today."
"I'm doing the best I can."
"There's a lot of other people in front of you."
"There's a lot of other people with the same..."
"I'm either on my phone or away from my desk."

Any computer that answers the phone; Anyone unfriendly;
Anyone passing the buck; Anyone giving an excuse;
Anyone arguing...
is giving **HELL** to the customer.

What are *you* giving?

Introducing the Customer (HELP!) 02

Shouldn't it *really*
be called

"CUSTOMER HELPING"

rather than
"customer service"?

AND
wouldn't you deliver
better service
if you thought of it
that way?

What else would customers like?

Value
"I want to know that what I'm buying is at a fair price, and will be supported throughout the length of my ownership."

Communication
"Let me know what I need to know, when I need to know it."

Attitude
"Happy, eager, willing... prepared to meet my needs."

Reliability
"Consistent...be there when I need you."

Tangibility
"Quality of product and performance... professional image."

Assurance
"Deliver when you promised... total product knowledge."

Empathy
"Understand me and my needs. Give me your commitment."

Exceptional Service
"I vote with my money, and an election is held every time I want to re-order or tell a friend."

☛ Know me

☛ Understand me

☛ Lead me

☛ Help me

☛ Serve me

the way I expect to be served...

NOW!

Let's define your customer...

overbearing

demanding

cheap

past due

back stabbing

wolf crying

disloyal

lying

one more thing...

PAYCHECK!

The president, CEO, or owner of your company

does not pay you. He or she is just a conduit for funds.

The customer pays you.

The boss just writes the checks for money

put in the bank by customers.

It's not your boss you need to be afraid to make angry...

it's your customer.

When your company's cash flow can't make payroll --
the CEO doesn't run home and break his piggyback to meet
the obligation. Rather he screams --
"Collect more money! -- Make more sales!"

GetReal...

Your kids eat
because customers buy!

Want a new telephone greeting?
"Hello, ABC Manufacturing, thanks for the food!")

JustTryThis...

Here's a way to ensure you understand who the customer is. Every time you lose a customer, and he stops doing business with your company -- the net result from the loss of revenue is...

your kids eat less!

To combat this -- go home tonight and at the dinner table, take a picture of your children -- *eating*.

Make duplicate copies of the picture
and post them
on the dashboard of your car,
your telephone,
and your computer screen.

If you don't have any children,
go home to your parents' house
and let them take a picture of YOU eating --
same thing.

WHAT'S ONE CUSTOMER WORTH?

*If you lose one,
multiply one customer's annual
sales volume x 20 years!*

WOW!

 ...

*How many customers
have you lost this month?
How many dollars
does that translate into?*

The **challenge** for the 21st century is not *just* serving customers...

- It's understanding customers.

- It's being prepared to serve customers.

- It's helping an angry customer *immediately*.

- It's asking customers for information.

- It's listening to customers.

- It's being responsible for your actions when a customer calls.

- It's living up to your commitments.

- It's being memorable.

- It's surprising customers.

- It's striving to keep customers for life.

- It's getting unsolicited referrals from customers...*regularly!*

Every time a customer calls or you call a customer -- you have an opportunity *and* a choice.

What choice are you making?

 ...

Are you creating frequent, lasting, memorable impressions?

JustTryThis ...

Name one.

Treat *every* customer as though they were your favorite celebrity, hero, friend, neighbor, or **your grandma**.

How else might you think of your customer?

03

THE REALITY OF SERVICE -- LOUSY, SATISFACTORY, OR MEMORABLE?

- The "Ladder" of Customer Service
- Lousy Service --
  all our representatives are busy now, get in line
- Loyalty.
  What is it? How do you get it?
- Satisfied or loyal --
  which are your customers?

THE "LADDER" OF CUSTOMER SERVICE

	THE CUSTOMER IS...	TELLS?	REFERS?	BUYS AGAIN?
top rung	**LOYAL**	tells everyone about you	refers everyone proactively	always returns to buy
middle rung	very satisfied	tells a few people	refers a few people	sometimes returns
lowest rung	satisfied	may tell someone, if asked	if asked, may refer	if convenient, may buy
	UNDERGROUND LEVEL	L O W E S T A C C E P T A B L E L E V E L		
one rung under	apathetic	tells no one	likely no one	maybe yes, probably not
bell rung	unhappy	tells at least 10 people	for sure no one	after a few years -- maybe
rung wrong	did wrong	tells at least 25 people	absolutely no one	only by force
dumb rung	pissed	tells everyone who will listen	surely you jest	never -- or when it snows in hell
all rung out	law suit	tells the whole city	(reverse referral) anyone BUT you	not even if it helps the space program

There is no higher level of achievement
(rung on the ladder) than LOYALTY.
Satisfied is the lowest acceptable level
(rung) of service offerings.
The underground rungs are shown because
it's necessary to understand that if your service
is at these levels, you are lower than dirt
in the eyes of your customer,
and all of their friends --
your potential referred new customers.

"ALL OUR REPRESENTATIVES ARE BUSY NOW, GET IN LINE."

Lousy service.

We all get it, and get mad. The real question is --
are you giving it? "Of course not," you say. "Not our company,
we give great service." My answer is two words -- "Wanna bet?"

Making customer service "real" is the challenge of this decade.

Corporate America spends billions of dollars to train employees
in "customer service." The problem is that the lesson gets lost
somewhere between the training room and the on-the-job
execution. It's not that people who serve don't know what to
do -- they just don't know how to do it.

As I travel the country, I'm exposed to all kinds of businesses
every day. For the most part I find service to be average or below.
Excellent service is rare.

Another personal observation is -- the bigger the company, the
worse the service. Employees of big companies (with some rare
exceptions) tend to be non-caring, butt-covering, work 9 to 5,
"it's not my job," "it's someone else's fault," kind of people. And
worse, their "vice presidents-in-charge-of-dumb-moves" have
decided to completely eliminate human beings from answering
the phone.

Automatic voice attendants are the scourge of American business --
most lead you to infinite hold -- and every single person (customer)
who has to endure it, hates it -- and the company it's attached to.

It's actually a good thing this crap exists, because it gives small
entrepreneurs a chance to nibble some business away from the
big boys -- and they do.

In my business experience, I've encountered hundreds of horrible
experiences (that turn into stories) from directory assistance, on-line
computer services, airlines, pizza delivery, major hotel chains, airport
car rentals, power company "customer service" departments, the
phone company, "service departments" at automobile dealers, and
so on into the night. Lousy service knows no bounds.

03

The Reality of Service -- *Lousy, Satisfactory, or Memorable?*

I'm not talking little inconveniences -- I'm talking full-blown problems caused by people who have a chip on their shoulder, and get indignant when a customer gets mad. I love it when they say, "They don't pay me enough to listen to this." They don't get the fact that if it weren't for customers, there would be no pay. Customers are the ones who pay (you).

I've also had great experiences -- lots of them. But mostly from small companies. Like the owner of Telephone Answering Service (my answering service in Charlotte), J.W. Lee called me personally last week at my hotel in Toronto to tell me my messages couldn't be paged to Canada -- and asked me how I'd like them handled until I returned. WOW. That's service.

It's not the employee's fault, it's the company's fault for poor training, dumb management decisions that reduce service levels for the sake of profit they were unable to make elsewhere (I wonder why), failure to understand what customers want, and failure to hire happy people.

Now there are exceptions. But if you're reading this and think it's not you -- you're dead wrong. Poor service is everywhere. Good service is so rare that books are written telling of isolated instances of memorable service and they sell millions of copies.

The words *"Your call will be answered in the order it was received"* are the biggest insult you can give to a customer. The translation is "Get in line like everyone else, pal -- we'll answer it when we get around to it."

Walk into a bank, hotel, or any place where you stand in line waiting to be served, and the clerk (who is often representing a multi-billion dollar company) greets you (his life's blood) with the friendly "NEXT" or "Who's next?" or "Over here."

I love checking into a hotel after a three-hour plane delay in the rain, and the front desk clerk greets me with their new slogan -- "I'll be with you in just a second." Man, that's what I call a greeting.

When this happens to you -- don't shoot the messenger. Shoot the person who trained the messenger.

What's the solution? -- Stay tuned...

LOYALTY. WHAT IS IT? HOW DO YOU GET IT?

By giving it first.

Loyalty is an interesting subject in our society. One is loyal to one's team or to one's family, mother, and father. Loyal to one's spouse, at least in the beginning. But, how do you breed a loyal customer? Easier than you think.

In my experience, I have found that the best way to get loyalty is to give loyalty or take loyal action. Be loyal. The more loyal you show someone you are, the more likely they are to be loyal back to you. The best way to get loyalty is to earn it.

Loyalty isn't just something that's given away for nothing.

If you take the institution of marriage in the United States or any-where in the world, loyalty is something that is given at the time you make a pledge. To remain loyal until death do us part.

But, in about seventy-five percent of the cases, this does not happen and I guess, if you're looking for customer loyalty, you should at least start out at home. The reason most marriages fail in the loyalty factor is that the other person in the marriage fails to continue to earn the loyalty.

We somehow forget what it was like on the first day. It started loyal. Started out fine and perfect, but each day over an extended period of time, it wanes a little, wanes a little bit more, wanes a little bit more, and then finally, poof, it's gone. Loyalty doesn't disappear all at once. It erodes day by day. The same way you can continue to build it day by day.

Would you rather your spouse be just "satisfied," or would you prefer loyal?

JEFFREY GITOMER

And so, the challenge is: What actions do you take each day in order to be able to keep your spouse or your customer in the category of loyal? How are you earning loyalty?

(Get Real)...

We live in a society of "what-have-you-done-for-me-lately?" and as that relates to our customers, the definition of loyalty must be a daily executed set of philosophies, principles, and actions. Not the enforcement of a set of rules and regulations. Not shoving your policy down a customer's throat.

The Reality of Service -- Lousy, Satisfactory, or Memorable?

03

SATISFIED OR LOYAL -- WHICH ARE YOUR CUSTOMERS?

Everyone wants loyal customers. Everyone measures satisfaction.
I don't get it. "Jeffrey, 97% of our customers are satisfied." So what?
Satisfied people will go anywhere. Loyal customers come back
and tell others.

"I know," you say. "Let's take a survey and find out if our customers are satisfied." Wrong.

Most customer "satisfaction" surveys are nothing more than a pat
on the head. Pablum. Corporate butt-covering documents. *How did
we do? (fine) Did you enjoy your stay? (oh, yes) Were we friendly?
(oh, yes) Did we meet your expectations? (oh, yes).* Oh, no.

Satisfied customers are only a measurement that everyone did their
minimum "job." Big Deal. That's what they are supposed to do.
"Satisfied" (or "satisfactory") is another word for "mediocre." So,
"very satisfied" must mean "very mediocre." Oh boy, there's a
group of customers I want to have out there talking about me.

Customer satisfaction might be at an all-time high, but customer
loyalty is at an all-time low.

The interesting thing is, Corporate America is teaching everyone
that "satisfaction" is the goal. Somehow the corporate buzz words,
"total customer satisfaction," seem close to "total quality management," and we all know how successful that was. Duh.

If you took your "satisfaction survey" and added (or replaced it
with) one question, your report would be more accurate and truthful than ever. The problem is that it would reveal big holes and
major flaws in your "don't rock the boat" system.

The right question would separate the *great* from the *ordinary*
and give you a real report card. What's the problem with that? you
might ask. Well, if you're someone trying to maintain the status
quo, my question will rock your boat.

*Ask your customer to describe the most memorable thing that
took place during their last transaction with you.* I dare you.

Here are some examples of how to personalize the "memorable" question for your business:
- (*hotel*) Describe the most memorable thing about your stay with us.
- (*professional office*) Describe the most memorable thing about the way we answer the phone.
- (*office machines*) Describe the most memorable event during our last service visit.

As an example, what kind of response do you think companies that have computerized phone answering ("push one if you want...") would get if they surveyed their customers about "the most memorable thing that took place on the phone during their last transaction"? (Oooh, I can feel the pain of the daggers as I'm writing.) Ninety percent of the people who write in would express some level of frustration or dissatisfaction with the phone.

And the ridiculous thing is, these are the same people boasting 97.5% "customer satisfaction." Hello! Welcome to FantasyLand -- Have a nice day.

You can get a series of loyalty-breeding answers by adding the prefix word "how" or "why" to the existing questions on your satisfaction survey.

"Would you recommend us?" is a classic example of a question that gives you worthless information. The real question is "*How* will you recommend us?" or "*Why* will you recommend us?" Granted, it will require more work on the part of the customer to generate the answer, BUT -- if they were served MEMORABLY, they will share their answers with glee.

And when you get the answers, they are more valuable than gold. These answers are real information that will give you insight and direction to lead your company. And lead you to more loyal customers.

Get Real...

You must also have a large check-box at the bottom of each survey form that says, "Nothing memorable happened." For your total understanding of the loyalty process, "Nothing memorable happened" is the same as "I'm satisfied," or "I'm neutral."

The Reality of Service -- Lousy, Satisfactory, or Memorable?

"Jeffrey, will this also require more internal work to compile the answers of customers?" -- You bet. That's the best part. It will help every employee, at every level, UNDERSTAND the customer better. What a concept!

And for those of you whining "we don't have the time," "we don't have the manpower," or the ever-popular, "we don't have the budget." What you're saying is -- "I don't really want to know what drives my customer from satisfied to loyal -- or worse, I don't really want to know if my customer thinks I have ability to exceed his expectations of service delivery." Big Duh.

What you're saying is this: "If we're losing customers, let's just advertise to get more, or put pressure on the sales staff to get more of them." Bigger Duh.

And if you still think "satisfaction" is the measurement of your success, I offer you this simple challenge. I can deliver an army of 1,000 satisfied customers or an army of 1,000 loyal customers to your door -- which would you prefer?

And how are you sure which kind you have?
Biggest Duh.

It never ceases to amaze me that companies spend millions to attract new customers (people they don't know) and spend next to nothing to keep the ones they've got. Seems to me the budgets should be reversed.

(*but don't ask the advice of your ad agency --
they have other ideas*)

> The only four things wrong with customer service are: your perception of the customer, your attitude, what you've been trained to say, and the way you've been trained to say it.
>
> *Jeffrey Gitomer*

WHO'S WRONG? WHAT'S WRONG?

- The customer is always wrong! --
  and you're just about as perfect
- You're fired! By the real boss -- *your customer*
- What's wrong with (your) customer service?

THE CUSTOMER IS ALWAYS WRONG...

AND YOU'RE JUST ABOUT AS PERFECT!

It's not about right or wrong -- it's how you *react to* and handle the problem.

WARNING! The information below will be painful to read.

YOU'RE FIRED! BY THE REAL BOSS -- YOUR CUSTOMER.

Presto! Every customer returns for a second dose of whatever you sell or serve. Is that the reality? Or have you sold them once, and then got fired (and now they're being served by your competition).

You see, people don't stop doing business, they just stop doing business with you. Each of us has lost a customer or ten in our business career. Why? Lots of reasons. We all know what to do, problem is we just don't do it.

Being fired is not just maddening and frustrating, it's also an opportunity. An opportunity to figure out why and fix the problem. Here's a list of 14.5 reasons why customers fire you:

1. **Showing no genuine or personal interest.** Impersonal service. Insincere people. Commission (only) hungry salespeople.
2. **Poor response.** Take too long to get back to a customer or service a customer, and they will find someone else. People will even sacrifice quality for speed.
3. **Unavailability (people or product).** Formula: "Can't get the stuff I need, or can't reach the person I want, equals go someplace else."
4. **Hard to do business or order.** Long waits on hold. People who are not product knowledgeable. Computer voice attendant rather than a real human being to answer the phone, and going through three minutes of crap only to get lost or get put on eternal hold. *Bye-bye.*
5. **Unfriendly person on the front line.** It never ceases to amaze me how many angry people serve on the front line of multi-million (billion) dollar businesses. The first rule of every corporate policy in America should be one word -- "smile."
6. **Poor or rude collection practices.** This is a big one. Taking away someone's dignity when collecting a bill is common practice in businesses. Most have never taken the time to point out to collection people that keeping the customer is as important as collecting the money.
7. **Over-promising.** Customers are like elephants -- they never forget. You over-promise and under-deliver, you lose.
8. **Inadequate capability to handle the customer's problem.** Poor product knowledge, or too many service problems -- not enough service people. Double jeopardy if you make a lame excuse about it.

Who's Wrong? What's Wrong?

04

9. **Too eager to do more business.** (Too pushy, too much pressure) -- No one wants to buy more from a high-pressure person. Help, don't sell. Create an atmosphere of buying (asking about them) -- not telling about you. Don't be a pest -- have a solid reason for following up.

10. **Poor professional package or image.** Customers want to feel that the quality of their business will be reflected by the quality of those they deal with. How's your image? How's your package?

11. **Dumb excuses about why you "can't."** Customers are calling because they want HELP. They want help with *their* situation -- not hear a bunch of bull-ony about *yours*.

12. **Nickel and dime-ing.** Charging for every incidental like copies, phone calls, and interest on late payments, puts a bad taste in the customer's mouth.

13. **Poor product quality.** No matter how much people pay, they expect a quality product. If you're selling price and sacrificing quality, eventually you will lose the business to someone with opposite thinking.

14. **Poor service delivery.** Everyone expects fast service -- that's right the first time. How's yours? How's the attitude of those who deliver it?

14.5 **Poor training.** Don't fire the problem employee. Shoot the person who trained them. Poor or ineffective training is the root of customer dissatisfaction.

SUCCESS TACTIC: Make "reasons for customer dissatisfaction" the basis for a new training program.

What happens to angry customers? From a variety of reliable research, here is a compilation of interesting statistics:
• 91% who leave will never return.
• 96% who leave won't tell you the real reason they left.
• 80% will do business with you again if their problem is handled quickly, and to their complete satisfaction.
• When the incident is real bad and they leave, stories about what happened will be retold for years.

It's interesting that most of the time when we lose (get fired by) a customer, it always seems to be their fault. I'd love to have a dollar for every customer who was wrongly blamed. Ninety-nine percent of the time it's easy to assess who's to blame -- just look in the mirror. Your mirror.

I'll leave you with two questions -- What are you doing to build loyalty and ensure repeat purchases? Are your customers resigning or re-signing?

What's wrong with (your) customer service?

More than you want to know.

You'd think that, with all the billions being spent on customer service and training, service would be great everywhere. Wrong. Service is still lousy -- and in my opinion -- getting worse.

How come?

Big question. Lots of reasons. Lots of complex issues. Hard answers. (If the answers were easy -- your service would already be great.) Upside-down priorities brought about by a lack of understanding and delivery of what the customer wants and needs. And failure to make the customer the *hero* of your company policy rather than the *villain* of it.

This is compounded by the overall lack of responsibility taken by employees (from top to bottom) for actions that customers require. "It's not my job," and other issues of blame (the opposite of responsibility) are the biggest reasons why customers go to competitors.

Here are the 12.5 basic reasons service is bad (and getting worse) -- followed by "Get Real" questions. Try to read these without squirming. How you answer and follow through on the "Get Real" questions will determine who gets the re-order -- you or your competition.

1. Wrong mission statement. Your ad agency created it -- no one gets it -- no one knows it. It doesn't relate to the customer, it relates to the company. If you put a gun to the heads of your employees and said, "Recite our mission statement or die," they'd all be dead. (GetReal)...*Question: Why have a mission statement no one can recite, understand, follow, or live by?*

2. No written "principles" for customer service are established. Just a bunch of rules and policies -- most of which are written in terms of the company, not the customer. Principles are what you live by -- Policies are what you live with. (GetReal)...*Question: Do you have written customer service principles to guide your employees and your business by?*

3. Failure to start friendly. Give what you want to receive. The first few words set the tone for the entire dialog (maybe the entire relationship). The single most important brick in the foundation of customer service is "friendly." It is also the least consistent element of the experience. GetReal...*Question: How friendly is EVERYONE on your team?*

4. Failure to say it in a way that the customer wants to hear it. The first tendency of the front-line person is to make an excuse or tell why something occurred. That's the last thing the customer wants to hear. Customers want answers stated in terms of them and their needs. And that's rare or missing from front-line communication. GetReal...*Question: Do you have your "best responses" for each situation written down?*

5. Poor examples set by upper management. The ones who are inaccessible to customers and employees alike. It's easy to recognize them -- they're the ones who have their calls screened with the words, "Can I tell him what this is in reference to?" They're also the ones you can count on NOT to return your call. People more concerned with helping themselves than helping others. GetReal...*Question: How much day-to-day contact does your upper management have with your customers?*

6. Companies allow employees to be rude to customers and tell customers "no." When you deny a customer, their need still exists AND they are mad. Then you add to the fire by saying, "Don't talk to me like that." or "I don't have to take this." Good move. A complaining customer is seen as a "hassle" rather than an opportunity. GetReal...*Question: Who is allowed to tell a customer no? How do you handle, document, and react to complaints?*

7. We are living in an era of responsibility shirkers and blamers. It's NOT the department -- it's the person. It's not "management" it's a human being -- sign your name to your work and decisions. "It's not my job" is their credo. Responsibility takers are so rare that they often receive awards and have articles written about them. GetReal...*Question: Does the person who takes the complaint follow through to see that it was handled? Do you reward your employees for exceptional complaint handling?*

8. Companies are concerned with customer "satisfaction" rather than "loyalty." Satisfaction is the lowest form of loyalty. Satisfied customers will shop anywhere -- loyal customers will fight before they switch and will get others to do business with you by referral. Satisfied customers are apathetic. Loyal customers will be your advocate. ⟨GetReal⟩...*Question: Are you measuring satisfaction or loyalty?*

9. Low training budget priority. Big companies spend more money producing and airing ONE sixty-second commercial than they will spend on a customer service program in a year. They spend more money on "lip" service than "customer" service. Pathetic. ⟨GetReal⟩... *Question: How does your service program budget and training budget compare to your advertising budget -- or better stated: How does your advertising budget compare to your word-of-mouth advertising budget?*

10. Concentrating on competitive issues rather than competitive advantages. "Our price is too high" -- "Our market share is too low" are competitive issues -- (airline) customers want baggage room underneath row one and drinkable coffee -- those are competitive advantages. (The definition of a competitive advantage is: Something the customer considers very important, at which you or your company excels.) Competitive advantage is the most overlooked issue in customer service. ⟨GetReal⟩...*Question: Based on the new definition provided above, have you identified your competitive advantages?*

11. Companies make the fatal mistake of only providing "company training" and "policy (rules) training." They MAY provide some "customer service" training, but very few offer any "personal development" training (positive attitude, goals, listening, responsibility, pride, or communication skills). This is especially fatal for front-line people -- people who need to know it STARTS with positive attitude -- not the company policy or manual. Rule of thumb: Provide as much personal development training as you do company training. ⟨GetReal⟩... *Question: How much personal development training do you provide the employees who need it the most?*

12. Companies only train once in a while instead of every day. Fifteen to thirty minutes of training a day will make any employee a world-class expert in five years. ⟨GetReal⟩... *Question: How much daily training do you provide?*

04

Who's Wrong? What's Wrong?

GET VERY REAL...

12.5 Failure to realize who is really in sales and service: Anyone who talks to a customer (often referred to by mistake as a client, patient, member, passenger, subscriber, or guest). The accounting (billing and collecting) and shipping departments of America's businesses piss-off billions of dollars worth of customers every day -- and they do it without a clue (or a care) of what the long-term impact is to their company (and their paycheck). They're following *policy* without understanding *principle.* The policy may be to collect the money within 30 days -- but the principle is that the customer is your paycheck and should be treated with respect and dignity, so they will place an order another day. Do you have a list of people who interact with customers daily? GetReal...*Question: Do the people on that list understand, execute, and deliver the mission and customer service principles of the company in a world-class way?*

The above wake-up call is just the tip of the iceberg.

Next, you will be exposed to the *factors* and *principles of customer service* that must precede your company policy.

So far, you have just been exposed.

The Right Principles Create the Right Words

PRINCIPLES, NOT POLICY

05

- "It's our policy to..."
- The BIG DUH File --
  *"I wish I could help, but our company policy
  clearly states..."*
- The New Approach to Customer Service --
  Principles before Policy
- The 12.5 Principles of Customer Service Success

"IT'S OUR POLICY...TO PISS OFF EVERYONE!"

"Hey, you're in luck! -- I just looked it up in the policy book and it says right here I can do everything you want, just the way you want it."

What a joke. What a knee-slapping laugh that is. That incident only happens in one place: Never-Never Land.

Policy is written to tell you what you can't do -- and it's the single most annoying word to a customer besides "no" (and one is really just another word for the other).

Well, if it's so annoying, why do you use it? Obvious answer: It's your *policy* to use it.

Well, if everyone you say it to hates it, what can you do to change it? Now there's a thought -- what word or words can I *substitute* for POLICY that might be less irritating to my customer, my source of revenue, my paycheck, my food supply (get it?).

JustTryThis...
The next time you have to refer to the rules of
the company, use this phrase instead of the word "policy":

"In order to be fair to everyone..."
has a ring of humanity about it, and it almost sounds positive.

CAUTION: This is not a panacea -- it will not satisfy everyone every time -- but it's a better alternative than the one you're using now.

In any company I've owned, anyone who said the word "POLICY" to a customer was fired.

GetReal...
Do you like it when someone gives you "the policy"? Kind of sounds like "the finger." Wouldn't you rather hear "In order to be fair to everyone..."? Your customers didn't call to get a lesson in your policy, they called to get help -- and if you don't give it to them, they'll call someplace else.

This story is by Theo Androus, (AKA Dr. Dub), a seminar promoter and seminar leader. Theo is one of the best examples of "dedication to personal development" I've ever seen.

FROM THE BIG DUH FILE:

"I WISH I COULD HELP YOU, BUT OUR COMPANY POLICY CLEARLY STATES..."

Company policy. If you had a nickel for every time some non thinking co-worker mindlessly recited the corporate mantra instead of solving the customer's problem, chances are you wouldn't be reading this where you are now. You'd be reading this on vacation in Aruba.

This is the true story of how that simple phrase cost one salesperson $602.50 per word, or better stated, how the absence of "policy" language, and the substitution of "help," earned another person (a competitor) $7,230.

Having read all the books and listened to all the tapes on the subject of real estate, I decided to purchase a property that was FSBO (*for sale by owner*). This meant no Realtors.

I made my offer to the seller and as we neared agreement we both realized we didn't have an official (standard) real estate contract. So I called the Realtor who had helped my parents buy and sell a couple of houses (thinking that since this person had already earned considerable commissions, not to mention the relationship that was now many years in the making, she would be willing, able, and eager to help).

"Sorry, wish I could help you but our company policy..." After begging, pleading, and offering to pay cash for the contract, the best I could get her to do was give me a photo copy of a contract. (Have you ever seen a real estate contract, 5-part carbon, "press hard because you're making copies" contract, laden with boiler plate legalese after it has been passed through the copy machine? *Puhleez.*) Come on, lady -- I just want a contract form -- not the CIA files for the Russians. "Sorry... I'd like to help you, but...," she said with the sincerity of a hungry fox to a limping chicken.

Frustrated, I was relating this negative experience to a friend and this friend suggested I call his Realtor. Cool. So I call what turns out to be the greatest Realtor on the planet (Pete Crouch in Alexandria, VA) and tell him the situation. He responds, "No problem, I'll take care of it." At first I was nervous, thinking he must think he's getting a piece of the deal, why else would he be so nice, friendly and helpful. So I sheepishly remind him that this deal is sans Realtor.

Prepared to be "sold" on why I needed him, I cringed as he replied. What followed was the greatest lesson I ever learned about selling. He said his concern was not making money, but making sure I was protected. He offered to drop a contract in the mail, or if I preferred, I could stop by his office and he'd help me fill it out. *Wow.* Pete said he charges a flat fee for hourly consultation, but that he'd give me an hour for free.

The free hour turned into three free hours. He answered every question I had, coached me on things to remember, and I left his office feeling ten feet tall. Armed with the knowledge Pete had given me (for free), I quickly saw that the deal was not as good as I thought. As it turned out, I couldn't reach agreeable terms with the seller and was suddenly back in the market for a house.

Any guesses who I called? Duh. Actually, Pete called me first to make sure my meeting with the seller had gone smoothly and to ask if there was anything else he could do for me. Pete treated me like I was the most important person in the world...and he helped me before he helped himself. I was renting at the time I called Pete, I didn't even have a house to sell and there was no indication that he would make a penny from me any time soon. Yet he took his time to follow up and see that all went well.

When a prospect calls you with a problem, challenge, or concern, find a way to help even if it doesn't put money in your pocket right away. Don't utter the words "our company policy" unless they are followed by "is to exceed your expectations." But you knew that. That's why it's in the Big Duh file.

Principle applies here: Your friendliness and willingness to help are in direct proportion to your success.
see page 82

PS -- Pete helped me find and purchase the house I really wanted. He earned a hefty commission, but more important -- he earned a customer for life. I tell everyone about Pete and not only suggest they retain him, but I urge them to do so. *What do your customers say about your policy?*

GetReal...Which do you think went further -- the company policy or the PRINCIPLE of giving help without expectation of return? "Help" went $7,230 further. *How far will it take you?*

PRINCIPLES BEFORE POLICY --
THE NEW RULES FOR CUSTOMER SERVICE.

Effective customer service is easier to perform than ineffective customer service. But judging by the way most companies deliver customer service, you'd never know it.

Why? Lots of corporate "policy," lack of corporate "principles."

Most companies and their employees have no idea what customers want, much less how to deliver what they want. Customers don't want to hear stories or excuses, they only want to hear that you care about them personally, and what you are going to do about their problem right now. Here's the rub -- companies communicate (about things and problems) in terms of themselves and not in terms of the customer.

Customer service people give excuses about why they didn't and why they can't (stuff about them) instead of what will be done about it, and how to solve the problem (stuff about the customer).

When serving, the secret is "think other guy" first.

GetReal...

Why companies train employees ad nauseam about their policies is beyond me. Policies have nothing to do with success, principles have everything to do with the success of "people" -- that leads to the success of "company." To serve customers, a set of principles must be established so that the policies can be delivered in a positive, customer-retaining manner. Oh, that.

JustTryThis...

Try to substitute the next dozen "matters of policy" for solutions that will help your customer. Try not to say the word "policy" once. Listen for the results. Ask them how they feel before they hang up. Get a reading that it's working -- then keep doing it until you own the process.

Principles, NOT Policy

05

12.5

PRINCIPLES
of
CUSTOMER
SERVICE
SUCCESS

with a game plan and success steps
for each of the 12.5 principles

AS YOU READ, YOU CAN EVALUATE YOUR PRESENT ABILITY...

Thought-provoking

SELF-EVALUATION

*questions will ask you to rate
your present ability in each of
the principles.*

After you read each question, put a number between
1 and 10 (1=lowest, 10=highest) that best defines where
your skill level is today.

At the end of each principle, I will challenge you with
"Get Real" success actions that lead to mastery of the principle
and loyalty from the customer. A realistic look at the present
situation. And I will ask you to "Just Try This," an easy first
step to implementation of the principle.

YOUR CUSTOMER IS YOUR PAYCHECK.

Don't be fooled by the signature at the bottom of your
payroll check -- the guy who signed the check didn't put the
money there -- your customers did. No customers, no money.
You should change your customer greeting to
"Hi, thanks for the food!" Your business is worthless,
and your wallet is empty without funds
provided by customers.

☞ **THE SELF-EVALUATION** *thought-provoking questions...*

How do you think of your customers? Do you recognize that they
feed your family? -- Do you understand that your degree of service
and help determine your wage and your success?

LOWEST	1	2	3	4	5	6	7	8	9	10	HIGHEST

E V A L U A T E   Y O U R   P R E S E N T   A B I L I T Y

After you've read the questions, select (X)
the number that best defines where you are
at that skill level TODAY.

Get Real ... *The more you work FOR the customer's success, the more
you will earn. You won't get the money the second you perform the service.
Don't measure each action -- consider the entire picture. The better you
serve, the better you will eat. The more you do for the customer, the more
praise you will get, the more you will earn.*

Just Try This ... *Paste a copy of your paycheck (where no one can see it
but you) in a place where you serve customers. Look at it every time you serve.
Better yet, write yourself a check for a million dollars and put your name in
the "pay to" blank. At the bottom left of the check is a line with the word "for"
in front of it -- just write "fantastic service" and pay yourself in advance.*

Principles, NOT Policy

05

YOUR ATTITUDE

(THE WAY YOU DEDICATE YOURSELF TO THE WAY YOU THINK)

DETERMINES THE DEGREE OF EXCELLENCE OF SERVICE YOU PERFORM.

Positive attitude is the foundation of your life -- and the determining factor of your ability to serve. Your positive attitude has the best possibility of creating positive customer perception of your entire company. How positive (enthusiastic and friendly) are the first words spoken to your customer?

☞ **THE SELF-EVALUATION** *thought-provoking questions...*

How consistent is your positive attitude? Do you spend 15 minutes a morning reading positive information to get your day going?

LOWEST	1	2	3	4	5	6	7	8	9	10	HIGHEST

EVALUATE YOUR PRESENT ABILITY

After you've read the questions, select (X)
the number that best defines where you are
at that skill level TODAY.

GetReal...*How do YOU like dealing with a customer service person that's indifferent or has a lousy attitude? You'd better create and deliver positive first words before your competition catches on.*

JustTryThis...*Read about positive attitude for 15 minutes each morning for thirty days. Just a page or two from one of three books: Think and Grow Rich by Napoleon Hill; How to Win Friends and Influence People by Dale Carnegie; or The Power of Positive Thinking by Norman Vincent Peale. Then write down the best quote of the day. A sentence or two that inspired you. Take it into work -- enter it in your computer -- make it fancy -- print it out and put copies on everyone else's screen.*

The first day everyone will think you're nuts. Do it every day for a few weeks -- then skip a day. Fifty people will come over to your desk and say, "Hey, I didn't get my quote today -- everything OK? Where's my quote?" You can have a positive effect on your attitude and the attitude of your entire company with one quote each day and a few pieces of paper. WOW!

05

Principles, NOT Policy

CUSTOMERS CALL, CONTACT, OR VISIT FOR ONE REASON -- THEY NEED HELP!

Most of the time we don't give them help -- we give them hell. They can't get through without automated attendant, voice mail, or hassle. One of the cries of the mass consumer is "You wouldn't believe what I had to go through just to speak to a live human being." -- When the customer finally gets through they're already mad or exasperated -- and of course the response is "our company policy states..." and the customer boils over.

Customers will want to talk to you (and buy from you), if they believe that you can solve their problems (resolve their situations). If you gain their trust, they won't call the competition, and they won't be as price sensitive...They just want help, and comfort.

How do you think of your customers? Do you recognize that they feed your family? -- Do you understand that your degree of service and help determine your wage and your success?

☞ **THE SELF-EVALUATION** *thought-provoking questions...*

How do you know that the customer receives help when they call? Have you documented the BEST responses for every reason a customer calls or contacts you?

LOWEST | 1 | 2 | 3 | 4 | 5 | 6 | 7 | 8 | 9 | 10 | HIGHEST

EVALUATE YOUR PRESENT ABILITY
After you've read the questions, select (X)
the number that best defines where you are
at that skill level TODAY.

GetReal...*When YOU are the customer, you expect real help.*

JustTryThis...*Learn the top five reasons why your customers call, and develop the BEST way to respond to each need. Something that works for you, helps the customer, AND makes them feel great about dealing with you. Ask your co-workers for input.*

PRINCIPLE 4

THE VALUE OF A CUSTOMER IS 20 TIMES HIS ANNUAL SALES VOLUME.

A $10,000-a-year customer has a lifetime value of $200,000. WOW! That's what you earn if you keep him. That's what you fail to earn if you lose him. The key to success is to earn the next order during and between transactions with customers.

A service action or educational communication is as critical to the long-term loyalty of a customer as a sales action.

 **THE SELF-EVALUATION** *thought-provoking questions...*

Do you know how much one customer means to your company? Have you ever lost a customer? Did you calculate the cost of the loss?

LOWEST	1	2	3	4	5	6	7	8	9	10	HIGHEST

EVALUATE YOUR PRESENT ABILITY

After you've read the questions, select (X)
the number that best defines where you are
at that skill level TODAY.

GetReal...*Do you spend as much to keep existing customers as you do attracting new ones? I doubt it.*

JustTryThis...*Every customer contact is an opportunity to earn the next sale. Contact ten customers a day and just say, "Thanks."*

PRINCIPLE 5

A CUSTOMER READY TO REPEAT HIS PURCHASE IS A POWERFUL BUSINESS ADVANTAGE.

The quality of the relationship with your customers determines loyalty (continuity) more than the price of your products.

Have you earned the right to the re-order? Is it easy to do business with you? Will they buy from you? Will your relationship carry the sale -- or will your customer shop for price? A clue about re-orders -- you don't GET them -- you EARN them.

☞ **THE SELF-EVALUATION** *thought-provoking questions...*

How many re-orders do you get? What is the percentage of re-orders your company gets? How many chances have you lost?

LOWEST	1	2	3	4	5	6	7	8	9	10	HIGHEST

EVALUATE YOUR PRESENT ABILITY

After you've read the questions, select (X)
the number that best defines where you are
at that skill level TODAY.

GetReal...*A re-order sale is 100 times easier to get than a sale from an ad, or a sale from a cold call. What strategy do you have in place to stay in front of your customer in times of "non-sale" as much as you do in times of "sale."*

JustTryThis...*Include relationship-building strategies in every re-order. After you take a re-order, ask each of the next 30 customers "why" they bought from you, and what you could do for next time that would make ordering easier. Write down the responses and meet with others to discuss them. (Customers always have the best ideas to improve your business.)*

Principles, NOT Policy

05

WHAT ARE YOU DOING TO ENSURE THE COMPETITIVE ADVANTAGE OF REPEAT BUSINESS?

If the customer is mistreated or decides to test the competition, that advantage may be permanently lost.

These are the common-knowledge statistics quoted about dissatisfied customers:
- 91% will never return.
- 96% won't tell you the real reason they left (*even if you pay them*).
- Most businesses spend 80-90% of their ad budgets and marketing dollars trying to get new customers.
- It costs 10 times more to replace a customer than it does to keep him.

But those statistics don't matter one lick to you or your company -- statistics are about OTHERS -- I'm talking about you.
It's not about statistics anyway --
It's about quality. It's about reality.

- Customer loyalty is based on the quality of your relationship. At the time of the need for re-order, the customer will make a judgment about the quality of the relationship FIRST.

What are you doing to build quality relationships with every customer? Quality relationships are where re-orders come from.

"CUSTOMER SATISFACTION" IS WORTHLESS.

Satisfaction is no longer the acceptable standard of customer service. *Satisfaction* is no longer the acceptable measurement of customer service success. The standard and measure of success for the next millennium is *loyal customers*.

 THE SELF-EVALUATION *thought-provoking questions...*

How do you rate the level of your success with customers?
Do you rate how satisfied they are?
Do you rate how loyal they are?

LOWEST	1	2	3	4	5	6	7	8	9	10	HIGHEST

E V A L U A T E   Y O U R   P R E S E N T   A B I L I T Y

After you've read the questions, select (X)
the number that best defines where you are
at that skill level TODAY.

GetReal...*Just because they're satisfied doesn't mean they're loyal. Satisfied customers will buy from anyone. If I offered you 1,000 satisfied customers or 1,000 loyal customers -- which would you rather have? Would you rather give your satisfied customers to your competition or give them your loyal ones? Get it? So, how loyal are your customers? -- Less than you think.*

JustTryThis...*First, ask your 10 best customers what makes them stay with you so you can better understand what makes a customer loyal. Then, think about the people and suppliers that YOU are loyal to. Write down what makes you that way. You will be surprised to find that the answers are similar. Incorporate the loyalty actions that you found in your top 10 customers into your everyday job actions.*

Principles, NOT Policy

WHEN YOU'RE DONE SPEAKING WITH A CUSTOMER OR THE TRANSACTION IS OVER, THAT'S WHEN THEY START TALKING.

A customer will either say something good about you, nothing about you, or something bad about you. And the best part about this is, by your words and actions YOU determine what the customer says.

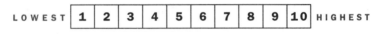

THE SELF-EVALUATION *thought-provoking questions...*

How do you think people talk about you when you're not there? What are you doing to ensure positive experiences for every customer who calls?

| LOWEST | 1 | 2 | 3 | 4 | 5 | 6 | 7 | 8 | 9 | 10 | HIGHEST |

EVALUATE YOUR PRESENT ABILITY

After you've read the questions, select (X)
the number that best defines where you are
at that skill level TODAY.

GetReal...*Customers don't make up stories about you or your actions -- you create them. What stories have you created?*

JustTryThis...*Select three stories you have told about others. Think about why you re-told them. Write down a few reasons you have re-told them. Now call three of the customers you handle most memorably. Ask them if they've ever told any stories about you -- ask them which stories, and ask them why they tell them. Compare those answers to the ones you discovered about you. Now -- start taking similar actions on customers that you think could be great (have big potential) customers but are not.*

Principles, NOT Policy

WORD-OF-MOUTH ADVERTISING IS 50 TIMES MORE POWERFUL THAN ADVERTISING.
(JUST DON'T ASK YOUR AD AGENCY)

One person telling another what to do -- what to buy -- where to shop -- what and where to eat -- where to live -- what to drive -- OR what NOT to do, buy, or drive -- OR where NOT to shop, eat, or live.

Memorable customer service (to create favorable word-of-mouth advertising) can only take place in a human-to-human situation. **Secret:** To be the best you can be for others, first you must be the best you can be for yourself. This means attitude, discipline, and self-education every day. Not "serve for the company" -- rather serve to be the best you can be for yourself.

☛ **THE SELF-EVALUATION** *thought-provoking questions...*

It's about creating WOW!'s at every ordinary situation. What's the word out in the street (industry) about you? How many people call you out-of-the-blue to place orders? How many people tell you positive stories they "heard" about you?

LOWEST	1	2	3	4	5	6	7	8	9	10	HIGHEST

E V A L U A T E   Y O U R   P R E S E N T   A B I L I T Y
After you've read the questions, select (X)
the number that best defines where you are
at that skill level TODAY.

GetReal...*America is not sold by advertising alone -- it is sold by word-of-mouth advertising. What's the word on the street about your company? Do you spend as much to promote positive word-of-mouth advertising as you spend on advertising?*

JustTryThis...*Write down the three things that help customers the most. Things you think one customer might tell another. Call your 10 best customers and ask them what they say about you behind your back. Write it down. Ask them WHY they say it. Ask them HOW OFTEN they talk about it. Now (the hard part) call ten customers you lost. Ask them the same things: what they say, how often they say it, and why they say it. Compare those answers with others on your team. You must take steps to eliminate the negative word-of-mouth FIRST.*

YOUR FRIENDLINESS AND WILLINGNESS TO HELP IS IN DIRECT PROPORTION TO YOUR SUCCESS.

All things being equal, people want to do business with friends. All things being not quite equal, people want to do business with friends. The best way to get to be friends is to be friendly.

THE SELF-EVALUATION *thought-provoking questions...*

How friendly are you? How willing are you to help?
When a customer calls with a problem, do you try to get rid of it,
or are you the person who solves it?

LOWEST | 1 | 2 | 3 | 4 | 5 | 6 | 7 | 8 | 9 | 10 | HIGHEST

EVALUATE YOUR PRESENT ABILITY

After you've read the questions, select (X)
the number that best defines where you are
at that skill level TODAY.

GetReal...*Think about how good you feel when people are friendly to you. Think about how it makes you WANT to do business with them. Now think about the last time someone was rude. See what I mean?*

JustTryThis...*Select your three toughest (unfriendliest) customers. Create an action plan to convert them to friendly by being ultra nice to them. Send them thank-you notes -- candy -- flowers. Things that can't help but make them smile. Get on the phone to a few service providers (vendors) of yours who are friendly to you and start probing about why they're so friendly. List friendly actions you can take.*

COMPANY POLICY IS WRITTEN IN TERMS OF THE COMPANY, NOT THE CUSTOMER.

It tells you what you can't do for a customer -- not what you can do. Company policy and customer service are oxymorons (direct opposites). Customers NEVER want to hear the word "policy." When faced with a policy situation, start out by saying --"In order to be fair to everyone..."

☞ **THE SELF-EVALUATION** *thought-provoking questions...*

How often do you say the word policy?
Do you use policy as a reason to say no?

| LOWEST | 1 | 2 | 3 | 4 | 5 | 6 | 7 | 8 | 9 | 10 | HIGHEST |

EVALUATE YOUR PRESENT ABILITY
After you've read the questions, select (X)
the number that best defines where you are
at that skill level TODAY.

GetReal...*Think about the times you "enforced" the policy of your company. How did the customer feel? How many times have you had an argument over a "policy" issue with a customer? And the other side of the coin -- How did the customer feel when you helped him and maybe "bent" the policy a little? Which of these two options will lead to future business?*

JustTryThis...*Review your policy with a team of co-workers. Rewrite a few parts that start with what you CAN'T do, and change them to what you CAN do -- AND how you address (respond to) the things you can't. Remember to insert the phrase "In order to be fair to everyone..." (or better, invent a phrase of your own!).*

Principles, NOT Policy

05

SERVICE IS A FEELING.

You know what it is when you get it -- so give back the same thing -- or more. The simple secret is -- don't give any feeling to others you wouldn't want to feel. You know when you're doing a good job, you can feel it. You also know when you're doing your BEST. It's an inside feeling of YES!

It's only possible to get that feeling when you're concentrating on building a better self. A better YOU. It takes a daily self discipline and re-dedication to your positive attitude every morning. It's study, it's reading. It's spending quality time building the character of the most important person in the world. But it's worth it -- I promise.

☞ **THE SELF-EVALUATION** *thought-provoking questions...*

How do you feel on the inside after each customer interaction?

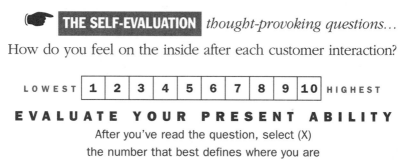

LOWEST | 1 | 2 | 3 | 4 | 5 | 6 | 7 | 8 | 9 | 10 | HIGHEST

EVALUATE YOUR PRESENT ABILITY
After you've read the question, select (X)
the number that best defines where you are
at that skill level TODAY.

GetReal... *Service is a feeling, and you know what it is -- whether it's good or bad. If you can't remember what "bad" feels like, call the DMV, Post Office, IRS, or Social Security. That's bad. Then call L.L. Bean -- that's good. See the difference?*

JustTryThis... *Remember how you felt the last time you got great service? Target five great customers and create a simple plan to make them feel GREAT.*

GOAL: *Try to get one unsolicited letter of praise for the way you made someone feel.*

P R I N C I P L E **12**

THE SECRET TO SUCCESSFUL CUSTOMER SERVICE IS...
START WITH...YES!

Instead of giving the customer a bunch of lame excuses or reasons you can't do what they want -- start your response with -- "The best way to get that done is..." or "The easiest (fastest) way to do that is..." Give solutions, not excuses. That's what customers want.

"The best way to handle that is..."
"The fastest way to get that done is..."
"The easiest way to get that is..."

👉 **THE SELF-EVALUATION** *thought-provoking questions...*

The self-evaluation -- thought-provoking questions...
Do you ALWAYS start with yes? Do you ALWAYS offer the solution?

LOWEST | 1 | 2 | 3 | 4 | 5 | 6 | 7 | 8 | 9 | 10 | HIGHEST

E V A L U A T E   Y O U R   P R E S E N T   A B I L I T Y
After you've read the questions, select (X)
the number that best defines where you are
at that skill level TODAY.

GetReal... *Isn't YES what you want to hear when you're the customer?*

JustTryThis... *Post the three responses above by your telephone (next to the pictures of your children eating). For the next week, start every response with -- "The best way to get that done is..." or "The easiest (fastest) way to do that is..." Watch the change in the way customers respond to you.*

MAJOR CLUE: *Institute a policy that states you must have a manager's approval before you can tell a customer "no."*

Principles, NOT Policy

05

YOU START IT...

you may as
well start
it positive,
friendly, and
enthusiastic --
no matter
what.

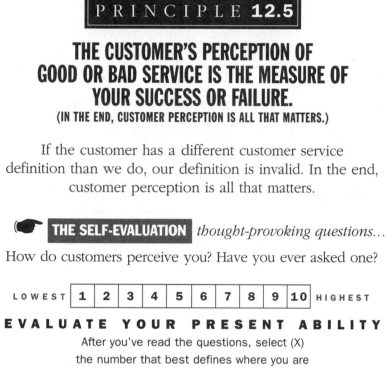

PRINCIPLE 12.5

THE CUSTOMER'S PERCEPTION OF GOOD OR BAD SERVICE IS THE MEASURE OF YOUR SUCCESS OR FAILURE.
(IN THE END, CUSTOMER PERCEPTION IS ALL THAT MATTERS.)

If the customer has a different customer service definition than we do, our definition is invalid. In the end, customer perception is all that matters.

☞ **THE SELF-EVALUATION** *thought-provoking questions...*

How do customers perceive you? Have you ever asked one?

LOWEST	1	2	3	4	5	6	7	8	9	10	HIGHEST

EVALUATE YOUR PRESENT ABILITY

After you've read the questions, select (X)
the number that best defines where you are
at that skill level TODAY.

Principles, NOT Policy   **05**

GetReal... *Master the elements of service that customers consider most important. How do you find out what they are? You ask them (duh). How do you master them? You work at being your best every day.*

JustTryThis... *Ask one customer a day WHY they like doing business with you. Write down the answers for 30 days and discuss them with co-workers.*

Do all you can to create good perceptions. Speak at trade shows and business functions -- get in front of people who can say "yes" to you, and deliver value first.

Test by measuring your own perceptions -- Be your own customer once a month. Call your company 10 minutes before you open, or 15 minutes after you close, and try to place an order -- or try to register a complaint. Or call yourself and listen to your voice-mail message. What's your perception? If it's great, that's how your customer feels -- If it's crap...

Well, those are the principles. Don't be discouraged if you read them and fall short of the mark. The biggest challenge is to Fortune 500 companies. Big companies struggle with principles within a culture of policies. This makes them more difficult to understand, let alone implement.

If you just tackle one principle a month, and get every employee in your company to understand it and work it into their daily customer interaction, you can beat any big company to the punch (and the loyal customer) any day.

And for those of you Fortune 500 people reading this and thinking you have the program under control with your customer policies and practices just the way they are -- remember it was you that thought TQM was good. What happened to that? Same problem -- policies before principles.

FINAL PROOF:

"Give me liberty or give me death!"

is a principle.

People are willing to die for their personal *principles*,
but I doubt anyone is willing to die for their *company policy*.
(*especially you!*)

But the best thing about these 12.5 principles is that EVERY ONE OF THEM CAN BE IMPLEMENTED BY YOU TOMORROW WITHOUT THE APPROVAL OF ANYONE. They can be enacted by YOU on behalf of (in spite of) your company. "Jeffrey," you whine, "what if I get fired?" What boss in his right mind is going to say, "You're too friendly! You're fired!" or, "You're talking entirely too positive -- you're fired!" Be principle driven.

SUCCESS CHALLENGE:

Become a master of principles -- *not policy*.
Act on principles -- *not policy*.
Live by principles -- *not policy*.

The word "policy" is over. **Forever.** Some compani just haven't figured it out yet.

Just a thought I wonder if the people who ma the "policy" e have to deal w a "customer" that it affects. **I doubt it.**

JEFFREY GITOME

THREE BIG FACTORS:
1. GET REAL
2. GET FRIENDLY
3. GET WOW!

- The "Get Real" factor --
  Your service builds or destroys your business
- I have no reservations about friendly service
- The "Friendly" factor -- *How full of it are you?*
- Memorable customer service --
  Where's the washcloth?
- Are you using the WOW! factor?
- The WOW! report card
- The WOW! factor -- **SELF TEST**

THE "GET REAL" FACTOR. IT BUILDS OR DESTROYS.

What is "Get Real"?

We've all had good service experiences and we've all had bad service experiences. "Get Real" is taking lessons from both.

Throughout this book you will be challenged to "Get Real." Reading the book is one thing -- relating it to your daily job functions is quite another. Get Real is designed to bridge that gap. Get Real gives you a way to think about the concept or example in terms of your job and how you can get better at it. How you can master it.

- **Get Real** means putting yourself in the customer's shoes.
- **Get Real** makes you think about how you felt when you got lousy service. (Remember a time when you were frustrated with poor service and the person serving you could care less?)
- **Get Real** is dropping the fake mask of "professionalism" for a minute, and getting real that the person you are attempting to serve (help) is another human being like you. Not a client, patient, passenger, or guest. A human being in need of help.
- **Get Real** is understanding that the person you're serving is some one who might be in a position to help *you* one day. Or a person who might know someone who might be in a position to help *you* someday.
- **Get Real**. If all it takes is an angry stranger to ruin your day, what are you going to do if something really serious happens? Why give someone else control of your life like that?
- **Get Real** is about you and the things you do and the things you think about.
- **Get Real** is a chance to focus on your actions and put things into a realistic perspective.
- **Get Real** is designed to make you see things as they really are, and challenge you to see them in a new way.
- **Get Real** will help you feel better about how you think, and lead you to pathways of solution or resolve.
- **Get Real** will help you realize that you're not alone in the mire of service problems.
- **Get Real** is help, real help.
- **Get Real** is real.

- **Get Real.**

I HAVE NO RESERVATIONS ABOUT FRIENDLY SERVICE.

I was calling to check on reservations for my one-night (*city un-named*) stay. Our office was closed for the holidays, and I couldn't find the information I needed (if you've ever seen my office, you'd understand). I knew it was one of two places -- either the Radisson or the Marriott Courtyard.

I called directory assistance and asked for the number of both places. The operator had the Radisson, but could not determine what address I wanted for the Courtyard, so she gave me their 800 number. Rats. I hate centralized reservation numbers. They seem so impersonal. People walk you through a pre-written canned script (that sounds so unfriendly) so you won't take an extra second of their 800 phone-time, and then they give you a "confirmation number" that would fill a legal pad. Then the robotic person says, "Thank you for choosing...(insert any name, they're all alike)."

Anyway, for some reason Radisson was on my mind -- perhaps it was that I had just spent two perfect nights at the Radisson in Pittsburgh (actually Monroeville). So I called the Radisson first. They didn't have my name in the computer, so I figured my reservation was at the Courtyard. I asked the Radisson person for the phone number of their competitor -- the woman was (surprisingly) ultra-pleasant, and double checked that I got the right number, because there was a Marriott and a Marriott Courtyard in the vicinity.

Then she *thanked* me for calling. (Remember, I had just asked for their competition's phone number.)

So I called the Marriott Courtyard. This time a man answered -- I asked if I had a reservation at his hotel tonight -- "NOPE!" he said -- like I had just asked a dumb question, and he was doing me a favor by answering (at least that was my PERCEPTION -- and that's all that matters).

If the Courtyard guy had said -- "Mr. Gitomer, I can't find your reservation -- but I'd be happy to make you one -- when will you be arriving?" I would have happily made one. But to the person on the phone, I seemed to be more of a bother than an opportunity.

Three BIG Factors: *1. Get Real, 2. Get Friendly, 3. Get WOW!* 06

So, I hung up and re-called the Radisson, and made my reservation there because of one word -- *friendly.*

I never asked the Radisson their price, I never asked the services offered, I just asked for a reservation -- and gave them my credit card number. They started to give me the compulsory confirmation number -- I said, "No thank you, I don't need it." -- and the woman cheerfully said -- "No problem, the room is in your name anyway." *Cool.*

How does this episode affect and relate to your business?
Let me count the 6.5 ways:

1. When a prospect or customer calls, the first words said to him or her set the tone for the transaction. *How friendly are your company's first words?*
2. The person who answers the phone represents the entire company. *How is your company being represented?*
3. When a question is asked by a prospect or customer, it means there's a need -- and a buying signal. *How well are your people trained to respond to the need, and ask for the sale?*
4. Most companies think it's their people that set them apart -- *almost.* It's their friendly people. *How friendly are your people?*
5. People prefer to buy from people they like. *How well are you liked?*
6. Friendly makes money, unfriendly chases money away. *How much money is unfriendly costing you?*
6.5 Whatever you say to a customer (good or bad) leads to word-of-mouth advertising. *What's the word out on you?*

A medium-sized hotel gets hundreds of calls a day. If only two people a day make a "friendly decision" at $100 a day each (as I did), that would represent an annual revenue gain (or loss) of $73,000. Wow!

What does friendly mean to you? To me it means smiling -- all the way to the bank.

GetReal *... People hope for friendly, but rarely get it. You can capture business with friendship gestures. You can lose business without them.*

JustTryThis *... Select a new greeting that's more friendly than the one you're using now. See how many people you can make smile at you in a day. Make a stick figure count of every smile you get. At the end of the day add them up -- it will make you smile.*

THE "FRIENDLY" FACTOR: HOW FULL OF IT ARE YOU?

How important is friendly? To me, if there are 100 qualities of a successful customer service person or salesperson -- friendly is in the top three, and may be the top one.

- Friendly makes sales -- *and friendly generates repeat business.*
- Friendly is a quality, and like all qualities, has varying levels of competency.
- Friendly is a degree. What's the temperature of friendly in your place of business? Is it warm or cold where you work?

And hey, if the degree of friendly in your place of business is somewhere between medium and *un*(friendly), here's a question that will make you squirm: *What's the relationship between friendly staff and loyal customers?* Answer: one breeds the other.

Well, if friendly is so important, Jeffrey, then why isn't everyone friendly? Good question. It seems so easy. One reason is that people are too serious about everything -- especially bosses, and they set the tone for the rest of the people. Do friendly businesses make it? Microsoft is friendly. Ask them.

The secret is for the corporation bigwigs (or small business owner) to create a friendly environment AND to train people to be friendly, AND to be (act) friendly all the time. *Friendly has to be "on purpose."*

Here's a 3.5 step plan that will make everyone so friendly, you'll feel like work is Disney World -- OK, OK, Wally World:

1. **CREATE FRIENDLY.** Select and document every friendly way, manner, and response -- then benchmark it (write it down), then empower your people to say ONLY that.

(JustTryThis)*...Have a benchmarking party for all employees, and let them participate in the solutions. They often know more about the business than the boss does anyway.*
- *Let your people develop "best responses" to repeat customer problems (late delivery, out of stock, error in billing).*
- *Let your people create "consistent friendly welcomes" to your customers (initial phone greeting, guests visiting the office).*
- *Let your people develop "best practices" for repeat customer interactions (phone messages, receiving an order, transferring a call).*

Three BIG Factors: 1. Get Real, 2. Get Friendly, 3. Get WOW!

06

2. **TRAIN FRIENDLY.** To some degree friendly can be taught.
   If you have grumpy people (or want to avoid attracting them), here's a few methods and strategies to remedy the situation:
   - Train people in the fundamental skills that build themselves first, and your company second. Most employers train about their own stuff and their own policies and procedures, but neglect the person carrying out the tasks. *Why try to teach algebra to someone who can't add?*
   - Train your people what to do in the top 25 real-world situations that occur when a customer calls or visit. Train them to ask questions that can close a sale.
   - When interacting with a customer, concentrate on the person, not the personality. Concentrate on the caller, not the call. *Your first job is to help the customer -- not yourself.*
   - Hire happy people. I have a quicker solution. Just institute this policy: *If you're grumpy, you're fired!* Simple enough -- no, no, wait -- better to get them a job at your biggest competitor -- that way when they chase business away, it will come to you.

3. **CREATE A FRIENDLY ATMOSPHERE ON THE INSIDE AND OUTSIDE. LIVE FRIENDLY.**
   - Be a friendly person on the inside. Have the attitude it takes to be smiling internally first. *Major Clue for employee:* Poor attitude can come from places other than work. *Major Clue for employer:* You can't change people's home life, but it's to every employer's best advantage to make the atmosphere inside the workplace a fun one.
   - Be a friendly person to your co-workers. Say nice things to them. Help them when they least expect it.
   - Create a happy work environment -- flowers, posters, banners.
   - Start with yes.
   - Have parties.
   - Tell jokes.

3.5 MEASURE YOUR "FRIENDLY" FACTOR.
Survey your people, survey your customers, survey your vendors -- get monthly (anonymous) feedback. Ask questions that get to the truth about happiness. Get the pulse from the heart.

GetReal...*Friendly is at the epicenter of your business, but it's only a seed that must be germinated, and then nurtured -- every day. The value of friendly is beyond measure -- it costs nothing, yet it's worth a fortune. And it's the most contagious disease known to man -- catch it!*

JustTryThis...*Answer the phone like everyone on the other end is a friend you haven't seen in years.*

MEMORABLE CUSTOMER SERVICE: WHERE'S THE WASHCLOTH?

Two true stories from the travels of a weary sales trainer.

I flew to Hawaii last spring. First time. Seven hours in the plane makes a person a weary traveler. I was met at the airport by my host and given the traditional lei (necklace of flowers). Fantasy fulfilled.

Gritty from the plane ride, I enter the lobby of the Hawaii Prince Hotel -- walk over to the desk -- someone smiles at me -- says, "Aloha!", and gives me a hot, steamed, moist washcloth -- ah! Just the refreshment and revitalization I needed. WOW, what a great way to greet a customer, what a welcome!

How do you greet your customer?

Other than the price of the room, the lobby, and a few knick-knacks in the room -- very little separates hotel rooms. A hot wash-cloth stopped me in my tracks. It was a surprise -- an unexpected moment of pleasure -- something small that separated the Hawaii Prince from the hundreds of other hotels I've stayed in.

What separates you from your competition?

What made it memorable? It was such a small thing. But every time I check into a hotel I'm looking for the washcloth -- and disappointed when it doesn't show up.

Where's the washcloth in your business?

What standards are *you* setting?
What makes people talk about *you*?
What makes people look forward to doing business with *you*?
What makes people tell others about *your* business? --
Like I'm telling you about the Hawaii Prince Hotel.
Being WOW! -- that's what.

Three BIG Factors: 1. Get Real, 2. Get Friendly, 3. Get WOW!

06

ARE YOU USING THE **WOW!** FACTOR?

One of the most powerful aspects of service: being different.
What is WOW!?...WOW! is great service!
WOW! separates the EXTRAordinary from the ordinary.
WOW! separates the strong from the weak.
WOW! separates the sincere from the insincere.
WOW! separates the pro's from the con's.
WOW! separates the *yes's* from the *no's.*
WOW! is the full measure of your personal power, and the way you use it.
WOW! is doing what others can't (or won't).
WOW! is what you do for others in an exceptional way.
WOW! is the ticket to success. Your ticket.

Are you WOW!? Is WOW! a factor in your serving process?
How do you WOW! the customer? How can you do it more often?
Here's how to WOW!

You can measure how much WOW! is in your service effort by looking at the following 18.5 aspects (elements) of what makes up your ability to WOW!

1. **WOW! Friendly** Be happy on the inside; START with friendly words and actions.
2. **WOW! Helpful** Take an active role in helping. Don't tell a customer, "It's on aisle three." Helpful is taking them there, and serving them once you get there.
3. **WOW! Best** Take personal pride in being your best all the time. Not being your best for the company's sake, or for the customer's sake, but being the best for the most important person in the world -- YOU!
4. **WOW! Creatively Different** Think how you can change ordinary into EXTRAordinary. Your voice mail, your greeting, your questions, your everyday actions. (MAJOR HINT: To get more creative -- study creativity.)
5. **WOW! Funny** Humor is an instant bond. Don't tell jokes -- just look at the lighter side of things. (MAJOR HINT: To get more humorous -- study humor.)

6. **WOW! Truthful** Customers just want the truth. They're going to find it out eventually, so you may as well start with the truth -- even if it hurts.

7. **WOW! Real** (genuine) Just be yourself. All the time.

8. **WOW! Compelling** Your presentation skills are an important part (50%) of delivering a message. Join Toastmasters™ as fast as you can.

9. **WOW! Fast and to the Point** Customers and co-workers will appreciate an answer that hits a bull's-eye the first time. With instant coffee and instant tea, customers have come to expect "instant" service. The good news is, very few people deliver as fast as the customer expects it. If you are instant -- you are WOW!

10. **WOW! Enthusiastic** Enthusiasm comes from the inside -- from the Greek root word "entheos" which means: "The god within." The best way to learn enthusiasm is to play with children. They have endless enthusiasm. The best part about enthusiasm is that it's contagious. When you have it, others catch it. WOW!! (MAJOR HINT 1: To get more enthusiastic -- study enthusiasm. Read about positive attitude for 15 minutes a day. MAJOR HINT 2: Hang around enthusiastic people.)

11. **WOW! Knowledgeable** Your knowledge of the customer and his or her business is critical to WOW! Your knowledge of what you do is also part of the WOW! success equation. (MAJOR HINT: To get more knowledgeable, study your field of expertise, or stuff about your job, for 15 minutes every day.)

12. **WOW! Courageous** Take a chance. Be willing to make mistakes. Be willing to fail. Being willing to risk often creates WOW! for yourself as well as others.

13. **WOW! Memorable** To separate yourself from your competition and everyone else, you must take memorable actions. Have creative, new ideas. Do things (professionally) no one else would do.

14. **WOW! Long-term** Visualize your customer as a twenty-year relationship and take all actions as though this were true. *If you do, then it will be.* WOW!

15. **WOW! Manners** Think back to your mother screaming at you about how to act civilized, and do it. Manners are noticed either by their presence or their absence.

Three BIG Factors: *1. Get Real, 2. Get Friendly, 3. Get WOW!*

06

16. **WOW! Understanding/Patient** Take time to listen. Be empathetic with the situations of others. Take notes to show you are listening. Take actions that show you care.

17. **WOW! Confident in What You Say and the Way You Act** Be confident and you will gain confidence. Build rapport first and keep building it. Use humor, use humor, use humor. Act and speak as though all is well, and all is YES. Confidence is your assurance that you will "find a way to get the job done -- no matter what." WARNING: *Don't confuse confidence with arrogance. One works, the other fails.*

18. **Be WOW! Yourself** You must be a positive, enthusiastic, focused, polished, and genuine person from WITHIN before you can ever show it, or be it, to others. You must be outstanding enough on the inside to be memorable on the outside.

18.5 **WOW! Able to Get a Smile or Hear Someone Say "WOW!"** The report card is there for you the instant you are WOW! Someone will turn to you and say it. Once you begin to hear WOW!, it's an addiction you'll want to hear all the time. Words of praise that others heap on you will spur you to heights you've never known. That reward is more than enough for taking the action -- BUT being WOW! will take you farther than that. The road of WOW! will take you anywhere you can dream. WOW!

THE WOW! REPORT CARD.

One of the best things about WOW! is the instant feedback. The report card. The people you serve and the people you help will tell you and show you you're WOW! the instant you are.

Here are the things to look for:
- Getting WOW! comments on the spot.
- Getting (earning) a smile from the person you're helping.
- Hearing "I can't thank you enough," or "I don't know how to thank you."

- Invitations to help others grow their business (focus group, board member).
- Personal invitations from customers (sporting events, parties).
- Hearing "One of your customers was telling me about you and had very nice things to say about you." WOW!
- A letter from the person you WOW!ed.
- Repeat business from the customer you WOW!ed.
- A referred customer from the person you WOW!ed.

Anything WOW! breeds loyalty.
And creates a story that will be re-told -- WOW!

Get Real...

The secret to a great report card (getting all "W's") is being and doing WOW! because you want to -- because it's fun.

The absence of WOW! is also a report card.

Three BIG Factors: 1. Get Real, 2. Get Friendly, 3. Get WOW!

06

WHAT'S YOUR SERVICE WOW! FACTOR?
HOW WOW! ARE YOU?

Here are the 18.5 characteristics/words that epitomize a WOW! serveperson. How WOW! do you rate?

WOW! Factor Scoring
1=poor, 2=average, 3=good, 4=very good, 5=the greatest

1.	Friendly	1	2	3	4	5
2.	Helpful	1	2	3	4	5
3.	Best	1	2	3	4	5
4.	Creatively different	1	2	3	4	5
5.	Funny	1	2	3	4	5
6.	Truthful	1	2	3	4	5
7.	Real (genuine)	1	2	3	4	5
8.	Compelling	1	2	3	4	5
9.	Fast and to the point	1	2	3	4	5
10.	Enthusiastic	1	2	3	4	5
11.	Knowledgeable	1	2	3	4	5
12.	Courageous	1	2	3	4	5
13.	Memorable	1	2	3	4	5
14.	Long-term	1	2	3	4	5
15.	Manners	1	2	3	4	5
16.	Understanding/patient	1	2	3	4	5
17.	Confident	1	2	3	4	5
18.	Yourself (WOW! inside)	1	2	3	4	5
18.5	Able to get a smile or hear someone say "WOW!"	1	2	3	4	5

Add up your score and rate yourself...
70-80=WOW!
60-69=AOK
50-59=Not Too WOW!
15-49=DUD

Getting to WOW! is identifying weaknesses in the preceding 18.5 areas, making a plan to strengthen them one by one, developing the self-discipline to carry out the plan, and taking action to practice and implement the changes. You *can* do it if you want it bad enough.

Are you WOW!?
Rate yourself on these 5 Get-Real questions...

Would I say WOW! if I were the customer?	1	2	3	4	5
Do I have what it takes to stick with it, stick to it, and do it until it's done?	1	2	3	4	5
Will the customer be moved to tell others a result of my actions?	1	2	3	4	5
Will the customer go home or back to the office and talk about me in a positive way?	1	2	3	4	5
Do I epitomize the 18.5 WOW! characteristics?	1	2	3	4	5

There is a challenge and sacrifice needed to put WOW! into your life's process. If you have the fortitude to put the package together, then you must put your WOW! in front of the customer. Here are the final steps to incorporate WOW! into your performance. Notice that all are intangible.

- Focus on your customer.
- Put your passion in your actions.
- Don't ever let them see you sweat.
- Let them feel your belief in yourself, your product, and your company.
- Never quit.
- Have your dreams ever present in your mind.

GetReal *...In service, it all boils down to the one word customers want to hear...yes!*

Get there with WOW!, *and the sky is your limit!*

Three BIG Factors: *1. Get Real, 2. Get Friendly, 3. Get WOW!*

Everyone

has a

complaint department

but no one has

a praise department.

Why not

open up a praise,

problems,

and information

department?

Reflect on this

Most companies think

it's their people that make

the difference -- almost.

It's their friendly people.

How friendly are

your people?

JEFFREY GITOMER

Companies spend more than 80% of their advertising budget trying to attract people they don't know and don't know them -- and less than 20% (often far less) of their advertising budget keeping the customers they have. Why? Why not reverse the percentages?

If you would spend 80% of your ad money making your existing customers feel like king, you could get one customer to bring you another customer just like them -- by Word-of-Mouth advertising.

That would double your business and keep your customers loyal -- what a concept!

Reason this is not done? -- two words: Advertising Agencies.

JEFFREY GITOMER

WHAT'S THE WORD OUT ON YOU?

- "Jeffrey, I'm going to buy some tires today!"
- Word-of-Mouth advertising -- *Free Money?*
- Mouth-to-Mouth advertising

"JEFFREY, I'M GOING TO BUY SOME TIRES TODAY."
by Teresa Schumann

Les Schwab is a retail tire chain in the Pacific Northwest known for outstanding customer service.

Part 1 *My dad told me what to do.*
My dad always recommended that I buy my tires at Les Schwab. About a year after I purchased my first brand-new car (in 1988), I developed a leak in my front left tire. Following my dad's suggestion, I went down to the local Les Schwab to get it fixed. From the first minute I was in the store I realized it was different. Everyone was always running. They were fast and efficient. It took them very little time to diagnose the problem. Diagnosis: I had a nail in my tire.

They removed the nail, patched the tire, and checked the other three. When I went to the counter to pay, they said, "There's no charge. Remember us when you need a new set of tires." I thought to myself as I left, "I certainly will!" I was amazed. Having grown up in a small town, I thought they might have done this because they knew me. But this was the big city of Portland, Oregon, and no one knew me. They obviously did this sort of thing all the time.

Part 2 *I did it!*
I moved away to Dallas for a few years, then moved back home to Portland. I bought a new car and drove it for a year or so until one day I realized it was time to get new tires. I thought, "Les Schwab -- wouldn't dream of going anywhere else."

My friend, Jeffrey Gitomer, called up to chat. I immediately burst out, "Jeffrey, I'm going to buy some tires today!" He said, "Wow, that -- that sounds exciting." We laughed, and I told him I actually WAS excited to buy from Les Schwab because of the free tire-fixing thing about 8 years prior.

It's important to note that I had already related my "they fixed my tire for free" story to more than 100 people between then and now -- but today -- today I get to BUY some new tires from Les Schwab.

I pulled up to their store. It was pouring down rain. (It does that a lot in Oregon.) As I was contemplating my next move, this guy comes running out of the store to my car with an umbrella and helps me out of my car and into their store. Cool. I didn't get one drop of water on me. I entered the store thoroughly WOW!ed.

Once inside they asked me all kinds of important questions about how I used the car, and then gave me 3 straightforward quotes -- high-end tire, medium, and low-end tire. Once I had made my selection, they literally ran out to the service bay to get started.

Problem. They did not have the specific tires that I wanted. And, I needed to get tires quickly for a long road trip. No problem. The manager called several other stores in the chain, and located just the tires that I needed. The interesting part was that everyone he spoke with in the other stores knew him on a first-name basis. I got the idea they did this a lot.

Anyway, I was directed to the next closest store. Now, I know that this manager probably did not make a cent on my transaction, but you would have thought he was about to earn a fortune. The effort he put forth to locate my tires and to make sure they could be installed in time for my trip was incredible.

I went to the next Les Schwab store to get my tires installed and was welcomed with the same umbrella treatment. WOW, I thought, they are really like this in every store. My tires were in stock and installed in minutes. The price was reasonable -- but I was not there for the price. I was there for the value.

I can't wait until the next time it rains -- I'm going to Les Schwab just for the umbrella treatment. I just wish they sold women's clothing.

Part 3 *I told someone else.*
Since that Les Schwab episode occurred, I have told a hundred people what happened. Now I'm writing about it, and countless thousands of people will read about it. And I'm glad.

Jeffrey was so interested in what happened, he asked me to purchase the book written by Les Schwab describing how he does it. I wish all the businesses I deal with would purchase the book.

AUTHOR'S NOTE: *The book can be purchased by calling any Les Schwab store. Visit their Web site at www.lesschwab.com to get the phone numbers.*

WORD-OF-MOUTH ADVERTISING. FREE MONEY?

Customers don't make up stories about you or your business -- *you create them*. The customer simply retells them. How the story is told, and what the content is, *is up to you*. It's based on your actions or reactions, combined with their interpretations and perceptions.

These stories create the basis for the most powerful form of advertising known to mankind: Word-of-Mouth. It is estimated that more than 50% of American business is based on this (verbal) ad form.

You will go to movies, restaurants, and buy books -- or not -- based on word-of-mouth advertising. Doing (and buying) what a friend has told you.

When people ask each other for a referral, or a business reference -- it's given based on their past personal experience -- or what they "heard" from others. Other stories.

Here's an example: "Hey, Jeffrey, you fly all the time. I'm going to Dallas -- what airline should I fly?" You can respond three ways:
1. A referral -- "US Airways is the greatest."
2. Nothing -- "Well, I dunno, they're all about the same." or,
3. A reverse referral -- "Anyone BUT US Airways."

Here's an example of the *whisper-down-the-lane* version: "Hey Bill, I'm going to Dallas -- do you know which airline I should fly?" You will get one of these three responses:
1. A referral -- "You know Sally, my friend Jeffrey says US Airways is the greatest, and he flies all the time."
2. Nothing -- "Well, I dunno, they're all about the same." Or,
3. A reverse referral -- "I've heard all kinds of bad stories about US Airways, I'd say pick anyone but them."

NOTE WELL. If the experience was good, the customer may not proactively say something, but if the experience was bad -- you can bet your last dollar they'll bring up the story in the first 5 minutes of a conversation -- depending on the severity of the displeasure -- sometimes in the first 5 seconds.

The reality of the aftermath of customer service is the most real (and valuable) lesson I can offer. First, because it shows how one front-line person can speak volumes for a multi-billion-dollar company by creating an experience worth talking about. Second, because you can relate to (and remember) it happening to you. And third, the future of your business depends on it. *Oh.*

Word-of-mouth is certainly more powerful than a bunch of rhetorical ads on TV, most of which are so plastic they should be accompanied by vomit bags. Word-of-mouth creates a classic opportunity to examine how customers can make or break a business *after* a transaction has taken place.

If 50% of American business is done by word-of-mouth advertising, what's the word on you? The only real way to "get the word out" is to create memorable impressions and situations. Excellent service is not what you believe it to be, it's what your customer perceives it to be. *And tells others.*

How are you taking advantage of your service opportunities? What happens if you do? *Here are 7.5 advantages of great service:*
1. It's free. Great service costs little or nothing -- but it's worth a fortune.
2. It builds goodwill. Consistent service creates and builds reputation.
3. It builds customer loyalty. People will actually look forward to the next time they do business with you. They're happy to do business with you.
4. It creates memorable experiences that will be retold time after time. Stories are the basis of word-of-mouth advertising.
5. It makes your customers salespeople for your business. And they are one thousand times more effective than any salesperson on your payroll.
6. It leads to referred business. People are guided and influenced by the success, satisfaction, and happiness of others.
7. It makes it harder (impossible) for competitors to steal away customers -- even at a lower price. "Loyalty through extra-ordinary service" is a powerful -- yet overlooked motto in business today.
7.5 It creates a clear distinction between two companies engaged in the same business. Yours and your biggest competitor.

AND people will tell others!

GetReal *...Every time a customer calls you, or you call a customer, you have an opportunity and a choice to be great. What opportunity are you taking? What choice are you making? Has anyone ever told a great story about something you did on the job?*

DOES YOUR BUSINESS NEED A BREATH OF FRESH REFERRALS?...

Positive
Mouth-to-Mouth
Advertising!

(the best way of breathing new life
into your business)

...

Who is giving you mouth to mouth?

08

THE

(SECRET)

SERVICE SUCCESS FORMULA

Self-evaluation is the foundation of new perspectives and positive transformation.

Most people think they already know everything.

This is a strategic advantage for the few who realize that learning is an everyday occurrence.

I don't care if you know it -- I care how good you are at it.

JEFFREY GITOMER

• The Formula for Successful Customer Service --
SELF TEST

The SELF-TEST formula for successful customer service has been discovered.

So has the formula for reducing the risk of heart attack. They have the same problem -- only one in twenty who know the formula will do anything about it. *Knowing and doing are not the same.*

Your ability to achieve excellence in these individual elements will make your service memorable service -- and that will lead to your success. *Here's the list, Rate your ability to DO the following elements. PUT A NUMBER FROM 1 TO 5 IN THE BOX ON THE LEFT.* (*1=poor, 2=average, 3=good, 4=very good, 5=the greatest*)

1. Be friendly first. Service starts with a friendly person with a friendly smile, who offers friendly words first. *How friendly are you?*

2. Attitude precedes service. Your positive mental attitude is the basis for the way you act and react to people. "You become what you think about" is the foundation of your actions and reactions. *What are your thoughts? Positive all the time? How are you guiding them?*

3. Your first words set the tone. All encounters with customers and prospects are yours to control. The first words you deliver sets the tone for the encounter. *What word and tone choices are you making?*

4. There are 12 elements that make great service possible. (None of which have ever been taught in school.) Establishing and maintaining a POSITIVE ATTITUDE; Establishing and achieving GOALS; UNDERSTANDING yourself, your co-workers and your customer; Having PRIDE in yourself, your company, and what you do; Taking RESPONSIBILITY for your actions, what happens to you, and the success of your company; LISTENING with the intent to understand; COMMUNICATING to be understood; Embracing CHANGE as a natural progression of things and of life; Establishing, building, and maintaining RELATIONSHIPS; Gaining the ability to make effective DECISIONS...(which means taking risks); Learning to SERVE others in a memorable way; and, WORKING AS A TEAM to make everyone more productive. In order to serve -- you must be prepared to serve. *How important is each of these subjects in your success? Have you ever taken a course in any of these subjects?*

☐ **5. Know what you sell in terms of the customer.** They don't care about your product or service, they care how your product or service is used to benefit them. *Are you telling them in terms of them or you?*

☐ **6. Know how to serve in terms of the customer.** They don't care what your situation is -- they only care about their situation, their problem. *Are you serving them in terms of them or you?*

☐ **7. The customer has lots of problems besides you, and may just be using you as a frustration vent.** Don't take it too personally if a customer flies off the handle. Use the three most powerful secret words that begin to diffuse all customer problems. *What are the three secret words?*

☐ **8. No one wants to hear why you can't.** Don't tell them when or why you can't -- tell them when or why you can -- enthusiastically! *How do you tell a customer "no"?*

☐ **9. Recognize customers for what they are -- your paycheck.** The boss doesn't pay you -- the customer does. Next time you think the customer's a jerk -- remember he's actually your next meal. Why not send him a thank you card? *How do you treat your paycheck?*

☐ **10. Don't confuse company policy with customer service.** If you have a company policy, fine. Never quote from it or hide behind it. "I'm sorry, that's our policy" is a chicken's way out. *Do you use company policy to offend customers?*

☐ **11. When you make them mad, it's twelve-to-one they'll leave or be leery.** It takes 12 positive impressions to overcome a single negative one. *What do you do to recover from an angry customer?*

08

The (SECRET) Service Success Formula

☐ **12. You are responsible, or it won't get done.** There's a fine line between taking it personally, and handling it personally. Individual responsibility leads to happy customers. *Do you take responsibility or try to pass it off?*

☐ **13. Take your job seriously, BUT don't take their complaints personally.** If you take it personally, you'll get upset and lose your edge. If you take it too personally, you'll lose your edge and your job. If you take it seriously -- it's you *with* them. If you take it personally, it's you against them. *What steps can you take to ensure keeping your cool?*

☐ **14. Your team will get stronger when you begin to build yourself.** Teams are made up of individuals who work together -- and get *their own* job done. *What are you doing to be sure that your job is being done perfectly?*

☐ **14.5 Customers talk to other customers and prospects.** Customers talk to other customers and prospects.

SCORECARD...

If your score is above 65, Tom Peters would be proud of you -- and your customers are telling others. If you're between 58 and 64, you're doing good, but you're still competing with frustration against the great ones. If you're between 50 and 57, you've got a chance to be great -- but lots of work is needed. Below 49, you're not a pretty sight -- you need make-up, and lots of it. The real remedy is a face-lift. Below 42 you need reconstructive surgery. Below 35, you've got 6 months to live, and it will take a turn-around and a medical miracle for you to recover. Below 30? You may be declared legally dead.

09

IF YOU TALK STUPID, THEY'LL GET ANGRY

(AND UNCOVERING SECRETS TO KEEP THEM HAPPY FOREVER)

- A funny and pathetic phrase
- It's all in the first few words -- or not!
- The Secret Words.
- More Secret Words.
- "It's our policy." Forbidden Phrases that your competition hopes you'll tell your best customer -- and other "never" words
- The BIG Secret -- *Put "Grandma" at the end of it*
- The Secret Formula -- *React, Respond, Recover +1*

How do you react
to an angry customer?

Here's a statement
made by animated voices of the 1990's.
They speak for the next generation of "servers."

"Customers Suck"

-- Beavis and Butt-head, 1994

It's funny when you first read it --
and pathetic when you think about it.

How do you view the customer?
And how do you respond when they get mad?

HINT:
Your response holds the key
to the word-of-mouth
advertising about you and your company.
And the key to your paycheck.
Oh, that.

IT'S ALL IN THE FIRST FEW WORDS...

The way the customer hears your words will determine his or her thoughts of being satisfied or helped. Here are the Prime Starting Phrases that will get the ball rolling in the right direction.

Say it the way you would want to hear it.
Just change a few pronouns or ask a question instead of making a negative statement.

JustTryThese...

After the customer makes a request or asks a question, or gripes -- before you answer the request or question, say things like...

Great!

No problem!

That's my favorite problem!

I think we can solve...

I'm sure there's a way...

I think I can help!

Yes!

Cool!

Can do!

Consider it done!

or, use the "start with yes" phrases:

The best way to handle that is...

The fastest way to get that done is...

The easiest way to get that is...

If You Talk Stupid, They'll Get Angry

09

BUT...

The next two pages
have the real secret words --
how to say them and
how to use them.

If you want to begin to
resolve customer complaints immediately,
just use these words *after*
the complaint has been given
and the customer has told you
the complete tale of woe.

AS A BONUS,
I have added the strategies that make
the secret words work.

The secret is in
the first three words.

The secret words are...

OH, THAT'S
HORRIBLE!

(said with extreme empathy and feeling)

These secret words not only stop the customer
from complaining, but it lets you begin to get to resolve
and solution. The customer does not want to hear
a bunch of your lame excuses about why it didn't work,
or didn't happen. They only want to know you CARE
about them, and what you're going to do about it --

NOW!

When you say "Oh, that's horrible," it immediately
lets the customer know you're on their side. The customer
is expecting you to provoke an argument, but when you say,
"Oh, that's horrible," the argument's over.
Try it -- the results are amazing.

*Here's three success strategies to ensure a great team
of responsible, service-oriented, customer-focused people.*

1. Hire happy people. Start with those most likely to succeed.

2. Record yourself and your co-workers once a week.
Listen to how you sound. Listen to your tone of voice.
Listen to how you take responsibility. Listen to how you
respond. Is that who you would want service from?
Listening to yourself is painful and powerful.

3. Take some kind of training every day.
If you want to be great, you must learn how to get there.
(Managers...if you want great people, it's your
responsibility to train them to be great.)

Three more secret words are...

YOU'RE
IN LUCK!

*I tried to make an immediate appointment
at a recording studio -- The woman on the other
end of the phone said -- "You can't do it until Friday.
We're booked solid until then. We can't take you."*

*It made me mad.
I had just spent a bundle there,
and felt as though my future
business meant nothing.*

*Couldn't she have just as easily said...
"Jeffrey, you're in luck! -- I've got a spot open on
Friday."*

Same message -- different language.
Much different feeling.

HOW DO YOU SAY IT?

Or... You could use
the "non-secret words."
The words used to chase
customers away.

"It's our policy,"
or other words that your
competition hopes you'll
tell your best customer.

A
BIG
list of words to NEVER say
is on the next few pages.

Pay attention.
See if any sound
(all too) familiar.

09 If You Talk Stupid, They'll Get Angry

FORBIDDEN PHRASES. HOW MANY DO YOU USE?

Got an angry customer?
Got a customer with a problem?
Got a customer with a question?
Got a customer with a need?
Congratulations -- you've got an opportunity!

"Hey, is that a trick statement?" you ask. "How is an angry customer an opportunity? Angry customers are a pain in the butt!"

Customers who are angry, have a problem, have a question, or have a need are the biggest business-building and relationship-building opportunities -- besides a customer placing an order. AND, (here's the best part), that opportunity is won or lost based on your words and the tone in which they are delivered.

What you say between orders, leads to more orders. More repeat business. It's for all intent and purpose why your business exists.

I've been observing what makes me mad... Probably the same things that make you mad. Here are the 8.5 things that set me off:
1.   Poor response to a need or question.
2.   Poor attitude.
3.   Poor service.
4.   Inability to get my problem solved.
5.   Listening to someone else's excuses about why they can't help me (why the answer is "no").
6.   Non-caring people.
7.   Inability to "get through" to a live human being on the phone.
8.   Inability to get help once you get through.
8.5 People acting like they're doing you a favor to serve you.

"Yeah," you're saying. "Those things make me mad, too!"

So, why do companies and their people do these things to customers? I wish I had the answer to this -- especially while it's occurring. Why can't there be some Star Trek phaser or something to zap a person into being friendly and helpful? Where is Spock when you need him? It's all so illogical.

It boils down to three things -- the words, the tone, and the intent.

The wrong words almost always have the wrong tone and the wrong intent. Here are the words I'm talking about. Here are the phrases NEVER to say to customers. Here are the words that your competition hopes you'll tell your best customer. Words that add fire to any argument, or just start one.

- It's our policy.
- What seems to be the problem?
- I can't...
- We don't -- we can't...
- There's no way...
- That's the way we've always done it.
- I don't handle that.
- Our computers are down.
- I can't find any record of it.
- What do you expect me to do?
- You should have done...
- It's your fault.
- Sorry, we're closed.
- We did the best we could...
- We've done all we can.
- That offer ended yesterday.
- (your voice-mail message) I'm either on my phone or away from my desk...
- I'm busy right now.
- That's not my job.
- What do you want me to do about it?
- What was that again?
- I don't have time.
- I haven't had time.
- Let me transfer you to the people who handle that. (Transfer -- you get voice mail. *Crap!*)
- There will be an additional charge...
- I can't help you without... (*your invoice, account number, a receipt, etc.*)
- We never...
- I'll have to ask someone else if it's okay.
- You'll have to...
- You'll have to ship that back to the factory.

- If you had just...
- Why didn't you...?
- You can talk to the manager, but she'll tell you the same thing.
- Let me tell you how we operate...
- I'm sorry sir, I'll lose my job if I...
- I've done all I can.
- The manager never lets anyone...
- I don't have to take this...
- Sorry about that. (Perhaps the worst, least sincere of all of apologies)
- You don't have to be rude about it...
- You're not the only one...
- They don't pay me enough...
- I don't handle that. (A variation of the dreaded "That's not my job.")
- Sir, I'm just doing my job.
- Sir, you don't have to yell.
- Please don't use that language.
- Sir, if you keep talking like this, I'm going to hang up.
- (Fake a smile and say in a sassy way) -- "Have a nice day."

Get Real...Your first response -- your first words set the tone for the transaction and the future relationship with the customer. Big responsibility. Big opportunity. It's so easy to do it the right way. Just select the right words and say them in a friendly manner -- and you win. HINT: Never use the phrases above.

Just Try This...
1. Start with yes -- *Give them hope of help. (Go back and look at Principle #12 -- Start with YES!)*
2. Resolve each problem all the way -- *Start with what you would like to hear if you had the problem. If you wouldn't want to hear it -- don't say it. The reward for problem solving is a customer who will tell someone else. The risk of not resolving the problem is a customer who will tell everyone else. There's a bonus for not resolving the problem -- not only will they bad-mouth you -- they will go to your competition to get it resolved.*
3. Say good-bye in a different way. A way that shows you care -- *"Great to see you (talk to you), hope to see you again soon, thanks for your business. If you need anything else please call me personally." (How does that compare to saying "Have a nice day"?)*

The "Grandma" (secret) Self-Test Has the Answer of Truth.

Here's a sure-fire way to determine how "what you say" will sound to the customer before you say it. A way to "test your talk" so to speak.

PUT "GRANDMA" AT THE END OF EVERYTHING YOU SAY.
What?

Every time you speak to a customer, end it with "Grandma" -- if it sounds like something you would say to your grandmother or your grandmother would want to hear, then say it. If not, don't.

How would this sound?
• Sorry we're closed, Grandma.
• Next! Grandma.
• What is this in reference to Grandma?
• It's our policy, Grandma.
Get it?

This is the best real-world self-test I've ever found.

Get Real...
If you wouldn't say it to your grandma, why would you say it to your customer? There are lots of phrases you use every day that irritate customers, and you have no clue until you insert "Grandma" at the end.

Just Try This...
Take the five phrases you say all the time and add "Grandma" to the end.

How do they sound? Now call your grandmother and run a few by her.

THE SECRET FORMULA IS REACT, RESPOND, RECOVER, "+1"

You do something wrong. The customer gets mad. You apologize and try to fix the problem, make nice, and hope they don't go someplace else next time.

Want to buy some "Customer Insurance"? Sure you do. How do you get "customer insurance, you ask? Easy -- you already have it. Problem is that most people (companies) don't use it. Reason? Insurance costs a little extra. It's called *Plus One Insurance* and here's how it works:

When the customer is angry, or you can't deliver the way they expect, the formula that will make them forgive you, continue to do business with you, and tell others about you is --
React, Respond, Recover, +1.

Here's what that means:

Let's say you're late with a delivery, or you deliver the wrong thing, or you make an error in something personalized, or you miss a deadline, or you deliver bad food to the table -- in short, you make a business mistake that irritates (or angers) the customer. Now you have to react, respond and recover from the mistake.

When you're done your dance of apology and making amends, that's when the customer STARTS talking. They will say something good, nothing, or something bad about you -- depending on what you said, how you said it, what you did, and how you did it.

IMPORTANT NOTE: The customer's story is crafted by your words and deeds.

How much is a positive story worth? How much is a saved customer worth? How much does a negative story cost? How much does a lost customer cost? The answer is "Plus 1."

All you have to do to ensure that the story will be positive and the customer will be saved is to add a "+" to the end of the trans- action. Something extra that the customer was not expecting. Something that will add a smile. Something that will add some "good" to the situation, and make a pleasant surprise the last memory the customer has.

For example, if your customer
- goes into your store for a sale item and you're sold out,
- checks into your hotel and the room isn't ready, or
- orders something and you deliver it wrong,

you figure if you just get the customer what he needs, you're
out of the woods and he's "satisfied." And you figured wrong.

You may be out of the woods, but you may still be in the dog
house. You need to add the extra. The "Plus." You need to add
a surprise. You need to add the memory. You need to add a
reason to say something good about you. Because the risk of
NOT doing it is too large.

Let's take the three examples above and elaborate, from the
customer's point of view. Let's assume the business can meet
your fundamental needs and recover from the wrong -- the real
question is: **What can the business ADD to the situation that
will make it a memorable one for you?**

Here's how to add the "+" and create a WOW!
- You go into the store for a sale item and they're sold out.
  *The clerk gives you a "rain-check" to ensure you get the item. AND
  (the plus) the clerk calls other stores, locates the item, and has it
  delivered to your home at no extra charge. AND (another plus) the
  clerk gives you a "private sale" card that lets you purchase anything
  else in the store -- today only at a 15% discount.*
- You check into a hotel and your room isn't ready. *The clerk says
  "Mr. Smith, you're in luck! Your room isn't ready. That means you
  get to eat breakfast for free AND (the plus) use our business center
  for free! WOW!"*
- You order something and it's delivered wrong. *The correct
  response when confronted is NOT an excuse. The correct
  response is "OH, THAT'S HORRIBLE," followed by a statement
  of what will be done and when, followed by some bonus:
  "Mr. Smith, you are in luck. You have qualified for our "Wrong
  Delivery, Customer Bonus" program. Here's how it works..."*

The "PLUS" is the difference between satisfactory and loyal. The
"PLUS" is the difference between positive and negative stories retold.

And the story will be retold -- the only question is which way.
I hope you're willing to invest in the "plus" customer insurance
premium. Some fools aren't.

The

customer's

story

about

you

is

crafted

by

your

words

and

deeds.

10

IT'S NOT THE APOLOGY THAT MATTERS... IT'S THE RECOVERY THAT COUNTS

- When something goes wrong,
  what do you say?
- From Complaint to Recovery
- The Personal Touch Method --
  How to handle an angry customer
- Angry customers:
  *How they get that way and
  how to calm them down*
- Customers talk

WHEN SOMETHING GOES WRONG, WHAT DO YOU SAY?

How do you apologize to a customer?

When your company makes an error, or a customer is in some way offended, and an apology is in order, all kinds of options are available. Most of which only make a bad situation worse.

How do you respond when something goes wrong? How does your customer service department respond when something goes wrong? I am amazed at the billions of dollars spent on customer service training, only to breed pathetic responses that further alienates, and deepens the wound that bleeds from the wallet of a customer.

When it's your turn to apologize to your customer for a perceived error, company wrong doing, or misdeed, here are the options:
1. Saying, "I'm sorry." The most often used phrase. *"I'm sorry"* are two of the worst words you can use in the English language. They describe you (and your state of being), not your circumstance. If I had my way, I would abolish these two words from ever being used again. *"I'm sorry"* is a state of being. If you say it enough, eventually you'll become it -- sorry. A more appropriate response is...
2. Saying, "I apologize." This is a better choice of words. It tells how you feel about the circumstance. You apologize for the occurrence. *Caution:* Many people say, "On behalf of... let me apologize." This isn't convincing. If you're going to apologize to someone, apologize on behalf of the most important person in the world...YOU. BUT -- *"I apologize"* by itself is weak unless accompanied by a solution (never an excuse).
3. Giving some lame excuse. No one cares about your problems or your excuses. Customers only want to know what you're going to do about it. Making lame excuses is *self-serving.* Taking action is *customer-serving.*
4. Blaming someone else. This is a lower form of excuse-making. Telling a customer it was someone else's fault in no way excuses the error. Customers don't care whose fault it is -- they only care how the issue is going to be resolved. No matter whose fault it is, if you continue to use this dodge (method of apology), customers will find your competition.
5. Citing company policy. Company policy is made for companies, not customers. The word *policy* may be the single most alienating word to say to a customer. Even if you must enforce it, don't say the word.

6. Saying, "Sorry about that." This phrase also means "up yours." It is spoken without a grain of sincerity. It is always said without looking the other person in the eye, and roughly translated means -- "Oops, too bad, I don't care." "*Sorry about that*" should be on the same list of banned words as *I'm sorry* and *policy.*

7. (Thinking, "Who cares?") This philosophy will put you in triple-failure mode -- you will fail your customer, your company, and yourself. If this is you, change jobs soon -- before you get fired.

8. Saying, "Oh, that's horrrrrible!" This is the most desired response because customers only want to know two things:

a. That you care about them personally.

b. What are you going to do about their situation now.

Oh that's horrible must be said with feeling and sincerity. Almost as if you were singing it -- and should be followed by, "That makes me mad too." and "I'm going to personally see that your situation is resolved as follows (give solution)."

9. Saying, "Thank you." This is a great way to begin a positive recovery. "Thank you for telling me"; "Thank you for having the courage to come forward with this"; "Thank you for bringing this to my attention" are words that will surprise the customer, if you follow up with the appropriate apology and action plan.

9.5 Taking personal responsibility for following up. Getting back to the wronged customer either by phone, e-mail, or with a hand written note will begin to rebuild lost good-will.

Well, which one of these are you? The best response is a combination of 2, 8, 9, and 9.5. You state how bad you feel, apologize for the occurrence, thank the customer for bringing it to your attention, take personal responsibility for it, establish a plan of action, then follow up memorably. The interesting thing is that only about 5% of Corporate America even comes close to this combination. So, by responding this way, you have a 95% opportunity to gain a competitive advantage -- *Try it.*

It's NOT the Apology That Matters... It's the Recovery That Counts   **10**

Reality Check: Business studies show that it takes twelve positive occurrences to overcome one negative experience. (Men know this -- it's why roses come in dozens.)

GetReal...

Do you believe what someone says, or what someone does? Apologies are worthless unless followed by an action plan, action taken, a resolved situation, and re-contacting the customer. Your first words, and the type of apology you first offer, set the tone for how the customer will receive the solution. Re-contacting the customer is the final (and most overlooked) step in a successful apology. The note you end on is the note your customer will begin to sing when he or she hangs up the phone or leaves your place of business. Act on complaints, don't talk about them.

JustTryThis...

Success Strategy. Even if you must say no, start with yes or transfer the customer to a manager when you are unable to say yes -- and try to partner a solution, rather than tell an angry customer no. Preface it by saying "The best way for me to help you right now is to..." Never say, "There's nothing I can do about that..." Let the customer feel a sense of help and support.

Big Secret to Success. If done right, positive recovery is the most powerful weapon in your customer service toolbox. State your apology and action plan *in terms of the customer -- not in terms of you.* They want to know about their money, their productivity, their lost opportunity, their aggravation, their loss -- not your situation, your excuse, or what you felt happened.

Easiest thing to do -- Just start to say, "Thank you," when you receive a complaint.

What tone (tune) are you sending (singing) to your customers?

GET A COMPLAINT?

When you take the call or complaint --
even though it may not be your job,
or you may not be the person who deals with
the complaint, you are the person who is
responsible to see that it gets done
or is handled.

Your job is to communicate it
and follow up afterward.

If you field the call,
it's up to you to be responsible,
even though you are not the person
who may take the action.

GetReal...

If you own the problem, you own the customer. If you lose the problem, you lose the customer. *It's just that simple.*

JEFFREY GITOMER'S PERSONAL TOUCH METHOD

HOW TO HANDLE AN ANGRY CUSTOMER

When a customer has a complaint, you have an opportunity to solidify your relationship.

The customer is always right. Except when he or she is wrong, which is most of the time. In sales, right and wrong don't matter. It's the customer's perception that matters. Keeping the customer happy is what matters. Keeping the customer poised for the next order is what matters. Customer complaints breed new sales, if you handle them correctly.

What's the best method of handling the dreaded CUSTOMER COMPLAINT? Try *The Personal Touch Method.*

Here is a formula I have developed and used over and over. To institute this method, you must first and foremost TAKE RESPONSI-BILITY, even if the fault isn't yours or you won't be the one who handles it. The customer doesn't care. He's angry. He just wants you to handle it. *Now!*

Here are 14.5 steps to taking responsibility when dealing with unhappy or dissatisfied customers -- and making them happy when the transaction is over.

1. Tell them you **understand** how they feel.
2. **Empathize** with them. (Cite a similar situation or tell them that it makes you mad too. Tell them a similar thing happened to you.) Comfort them.
3. **Listen** all the way out. Make sure the customer has told you everything. Don't interrupt. **Ask questions** to understand their problem better, and to **find out what it will take to help them -- the way they want to be helped.**
4. **Agree** with them if at all possible. (Never argue or get angry.)
5. Take notes and **confirm** back that everything has been covered, and that they have said all they want/need to say.
6. Be an **ambassador** for your company. Tell the customer you will **personally** handle it.
7. **Don't blame others or look for a scapegoat.** Admit you (and or the company) were wrong and **take responsibility** for correcting it.
8. **Don't pass the buck.** *"It's not my job."..."I thought he said..." "She's not here right now."... and "Someone else handles that,"*

are responses that are never applicable or acceptable to the customer.

9. **Respond immediately.** When something is wrong, people want (and expect) it to be fixed immediately. The customer wants it now.

10. Find some **common ground** other than the problem. (Try to establish some rapport.)

11. **Use humor** if possible. Making people laugh puts them at ease.

12. Figure out, communicate, and **agree upon a solution**. Give the customer choices if possible. Confirm it (in writing if necessary). **Tell them what you plan to do...and DO IT!**

13. **Make a follow-up call** after the situation is resolved.

14. **Get a letter** if you can. Resolving a problem in a favorable and positive way strengthens respect, builds character, and establishes a solid base for long-term relationships. Tell the customer you would appreciate a sentence or two about how the situation was resolved.

14.5. **Ask yourself: "What have I learned, and what can I do to prevent this situation from happening again? Do I need to make changes?"**

It is important to be aware of some practical realities when trying to accomplish the task of (recovery) satisfying the customer. They are:

❦ The customer knows exactly how they want it, or exactly what they want, but may be a lousy communicator and not tell you completely, or tell you in a way that is difficult to understand. **If the customer cannot state his complaint in a clear and concise manner, it's up to you to help him do so.**

❦ Remember, you're the customer elsewhere. Think about the level of service you expect when you're the customer.

❦ Every customer thinks they're the only one you've got... Treat them that way. Make the customer feel important.

❦ The customer is human and has problems just like you do.

❦ The customer expects service at the flip of a switch.

❦ It all boils down to you.

❦ The customer's perception is reality.

❦ How big a deal is it to try to give them what they want?

GetReal ...Recovery is powerful. *When you satisfy an unhappy or dissatisfied customer, and you can get them to write you a letter telling you they're happy and satisfied now, I'd say you have a solid shot at a long-term relationship.*

If the problem is left unresolved...the customer will surely find your competition.

Angry customers...

- they may have a health problem

- they may have a spouse problem

- they may have a money problem

They may be taking that out on you.

 ...

Take it seriously -- not personally.

A gentle reminder...

WORD-OF-MOUTH ADVERTISING IS THE MOST POWERFUL FORM OF ADVERTISING IN THE WORLD.

HERE'S HOW IT WORKS...

10

It's NOT the Apology That Matters... It's the Recovery That Counts

Customers talk...

to their associates, friends, and neighbors.
Here is the number of people they will talk
to based upon how well you handle
their complaint.

3
IF YOU DO A GOOD JOB

10
IF YOU DO A GREAT JOB

25
IF YOU DO A BAD JOB

50
IF YOU GET INTO AN ARGUMENT

AND -- IF THE ARGUMENT DEVELOPS INTO A FIGHT, AND YOUR LAWYERS GET INVOLVED, YOU WILL BE ON THE 6:00 PM LOCAL NEWS.

*How are your customers
talking about you?*

11

Most people

fail to recognize

that the

daily interactions

with customers

can be turned

into loyalty building

actions with a little

creativity and

a willingness

to step outside the

"zone of comfort."

Jeffrey Gitomer

BENCHMARKS SET THE STANDARDS... FOR BEST PERFORMANCE!

- Benchmarking Best Practices -- *The Best Path to Loyalty*
- Raymond Takes a Risk and Sets the Standard

"BEST PRACTICE" BENCHMARK -- A response, practice, or
function that, by peer consensus, has been designated as "BEST"
when interacting with a customer or co-worker. The function
of a Benchmark is to create a uniform, superior response to
situations that occur daily in the workplace. The objective of a
Benchmark is to raise the level of service and performance
to its maximum, and maintain that level every day.

Is that the best way you can *say* it?
Is that the best way you can *do* it?

Benchmarking best practices can turn an everyday situation
(greeting, responding, asking for payment, voice mail message)
into WOW!

Here's an example.
PRESENT SITUATION. Customer drives up to a hotel. Doorman
greets the customer, takes his bags, puts them on a cart, and
waits for the customer to check in. The customer checks in,
comes back, claims his bags, and a bellman takes them to the
room. Standard operating procedure at 99% of America's full-
service hotels.

BENCHMARK OPPORTUNITY -- take the service to a memorable
level. We'll call the practice "Name Pass," and here's how it works.

NEW BENCHMARK STANDARD -- Customer drives up to the
hotel's front entrance. Doorman runs to the car door, opens it,
and says, "Welcome to the Downtown Marriott. My name is
Marvin. How can I serve you today?" A stunned customer says,
"I'm here to check in."

"Great!" says Marvin. "And your name is...?"
"Jeffrey Gitomer," says the customer.
"Mr. Gitomer, follow me, you're about to have a great stay
here." Marvin leads me to the front desk. He walks up to the
desk, leans over, and says to the front desk clerk, "Amy, I want
you to take special care of my new friend, Mr. Gitomer -- he's
here to check in." (Gitomer, still dazed, hands Marvin $5.00 as
he walks away.)

"Great, Mr. Gitomer, we've got a great room for you, you're going to have a great stay here," says an exuberant Amy. "If you'll just give me your credit card, I'll have you taken care of in no time flat" (front desk person completes the task and calls over Bill, the bellman). "Bill, please take our special guest, Mr. Gitomer, to his room."

"Hello, Mr. Gitomer, I'm Bill -- the best bellman this side of the Potomac River. Let me show you to the elevator. As we pass the water fountain, watch out for the alligators."

Gitomer, smiling, puts his hand in his pocket to make sure there's tip money readily available.

Get it? It's so simple to change the daily grind into fun for everyone -- AND create memorable experiences that will be related to others.

A few examples of turning the ordinary into a retold story.
• Nordstrom's Department Store never makes you stand in line to pay. The clerk who waits on you takes your credit card and returns with a slip to sign and a bag for your stuff. WOW!
• Freedom Animal Hospital changed their telephone answer message to animals barking in the background and speaking as though they were a pet.
• Omni Bank in New Orleans took down their "no soliciting" sign on the front door and put up a "WELCOME" sign in its place.

IDEAS OF AREAS YOU COULD BENCHMARK AN ORDINARY PRACTICE INTO A TALKED-ABOUT PRACTICE:
Phone greeting
Receptionist greeting
Taking a message
The factory tour
The customer greeting
The initial response to a complaint
The customer good-bye
The customer follow-up after a sale
Word substitution

Benchmarks Set the Standards... *for Best Performance*   11

RAYMOND TAKES A RISK AND SETS THE STANDARD.

I drove from Charlotte to Atlanta and arrived at the downtown Radisson Hotel. I was tired and just happy to be at my destination to rest for tomorrow's seminar. The doorman, a dapper, slender gentleman, approached my car and looked at my license plate. "Ah, from North Carolina," he said, "My name is Raymond -- you're going to have a great stay here."

I said, "Cool." But, Raymond didn't pass my five-dollar rule -- if anyone from a hotel greets me with the word "welcome," I give him five dollars immediately. For the record, in 1996, in over 100 hotel stays, I gave away four five-dollar bills. In 1997, in over 125 hotel stays, I gave away four five-dollar bills.

As I entered the revolving door of the hotel, I was walking about five paces ahead of Raymond, and I heard a scream from behind me: "CHECKING IN FROM THE GREAT STATE OF NORTH CAROLINA... FIRST IN FLIGHT!"

I stopped dead in my tracks, and turned around to see if the governor had just entered the hotel. No, Raymond was talking (yelling) about ME. He was announcing me to the entire hotel. I was flabbergasted. And felt like a king.

I immediately took ten dollars out of my pocket and handed it to Raymond to thank him for best performance ever by a doorman. I looked at him and said, "So, Raymond, who gives you ten dollars?" He said, "Oh, pretty much everybody." We laughed.

Let me tell you a little bit more about Raymond.

I found out that Raymond made a great salary (the hotel did not want to lose him) and five times the tips of any other doorman at the hotel. I wonder why.

I did a seminar for the Radisson Hotel the very next day, and while I was speaking with all the managers, I told them that they had a secret weapon in their hotel. I asked them if they could identify it. No one could. I wrote on the blackboard, "Raymond," and they all nodded. They agreed that Raymond was a special individual.

I said, "You don't understand how special he is. Raymond sets the tone for every single guest who walks in the door. He makes every guest feel like a million dollars. You could make ten mistakes and it wouldn't matter. The guest is still on a high. I am."

For the second year in a row, Raymond was voted "Employee of the Year" at the hotel. A doorman who loved his job and made people feel GREAT. And as incredible as this guy was, he was the only one who did what he did, the way he did it. It was as if he had a patent or copyright on the technique.

Why didn't the other doormen do it? Why didn't everyone do it? Why didn't they make it mandatory to scream everyone's state of origin or people's names when they arrive? I don't understand it, but Raymond did.

Every business needs at least one Raymond.

GetReal...
By benchmarking Raymond's action as a "Best Practice," the hotel could have encouraged other employees (in their own way) to find new ways of memorably greeting guests.

EPILOGUE:
Raymond Guyton is missing.
I called the Radisson to interview Raymond.
He left his job after the Olympics
in the summer of 1996.

If anyone knows of his whereabouts,
I would appreciate it if you would
e-mail me at
salesman@gitomer.com

Benchmarks Set the Standards... for Best Performance 11

Memorable

stories

(good or bad)

about

the things

you do

are retold...

from a

customer

to a

potential

customer.

What

kind of

stories

are being

told

about

you?

There's a big

difference between

"knowing" and

"doing."

Self-evaluation asks,

"How good are

you at it?"

It's the gateway

between "knowing

something" and

"doing it."

JEFFREY GITOMER

PUT YOUR JOB SKILLS TO THE TEST

- The Customer Service Test --
  SELF TEST
- A daily report card
  is yours for the listening

The Customer Service Self-evaluation Test...

Will Hurt...and Help!

- This test will *hurt* if you take it honestly.
- This test will *help* if you use it as an evaluation tool (as it is intended to be).
- This test is the basis of your personalized plan to achieve greatness in serving others.

I have designed this test to point out an individual's areas of strength and weakness. It doesn't provide answers; it's only an evaluation. If you want answers, make a plan to improve each weak area and focus the lesson on a chapter or two from this book.

Go for it.

SELF-EVALUATION TEST

Commandments, Rules, Guidelines & Philosophies of a Great Service Person

How do you rate?

This test is designed to point out your individual strengths and weaknesses as a Customer Service Person.

Circle the number that best applies to your skill level -- **today.**

(1=poor, 2=average, 3=good, 4=very good, 5=the greatest)
(1=never, 2=rarely, 3=sometimes, 4=frequently, 5=always)

I recognize that my paycheck comes from
customers who buy our stuff.   *RATE* 1 2 3 4 5 ☐

IDEAS:

I act like today (every day) is my first day
on the job. *Impress everyone.*   *RATE* 1 2 3 4 5 ☐

IDEAS:

The customer I'm speaking to now THINKS
he is the most important person on earth,   *RATE* 1 2 3 4 5 ☐
and I treat him that way.

IDEAS:

I know customers buy for their reasons,
not mine.I find out theirs first.   *RATE* 1 2 3 4 5 ☐

IDEAS:

I smile!

                                                 RATE 1 2 3 4 5 ☐

IDEAS:

Put Your Job Skills to the Test

12

SELF-EVALUATION TEST

(1=poor, 2=average, 3=good, 4=very good, 5=the greatest)
(1=never, 2=rarely, 3=sometimes, 4=frequently, 5=always)

I'm friendly all the time.

RATE 1 2 3 4 5 ☐

IDEAS:

I show enthusiasm.

RATE 1 2 3 4 5 ☐

IDEAS:

I stay positive all the time.

RATE 1 2 3 4 5 ☐

IDEAS:

The first line I deliver sets the tone.
Mine is friendly and reassuring.   RATE 1 2 3 4 5 ☐

IDEAS:

I know customers are calling because
they need help. I help them first.   RATE 1 2 3 4 5 ☐

IDEAS:

I make sure the customer knows my name.

RATE 1 2 3 4 5 ☐

IDEAS:

I say the customer's name.

RATE 1 2 3 4 5 ☐

IDEAS:

SELF-EVALUATION TEST

(1=poor, 2=average, 3=good, 4=very good, 5=the greatest)
(1=never, 2=rarely, 3=sometimes, 4=frequently, 5=always)

I use words of encouragement (sure, no
problem, we can do that right away). *RATE* 1 2 3 4 5 ☐

IDEAS:

Even though it's my 10,000th time to say it,
I say it as if it's the first. *RATE* 1 2 3 4 5 ☐

IDEAS:

I use our products in order to better relate
to my customer. *RATE* 1 2 3 4 5 ☐

IDEAS:

I'm a passionate product of our product --
I study at night. *RATE* 1 2 3 4 5 ☐

IDEAS:

I know what my "favorite" products are and
how they are used. *RATE* 1 2 3 4 5 ☐

IDEAS:

I tell customers their options for more.

RATE 1 2 3 4 5 ☐

IDEAS:

I try to be a consultant. I make customers feel
secure about their choice. "This is the *RATE* 1 2 3 4 5 ☐
product/package that is most popular."

IDEAS:

SELF-EVALUATION TEST

(1=poor, 2=average, 3=good, 4=very good, 5=the greatest)
(1=never, 2=rarely, 3=sometimes, 4=frequently, 5=always)

I ask questions to create a greater understanding
of the situation: *RATE* 1 2 3 4 5 ☐
* Questions about their business.
* Questions about how they have successfully used us.
* Questions about what more they could do.
* Questions about what more we could do.
* Questions about their favorite product of ours.
* Questions to isolate their decision: "
  If it were only you, which would you take?"

IDEAS:
_____

I put helping customers ahead of company
policy (without breaking rules).   *RATE* 1 2 3 4 5 ☐

IDEAS:
_____

I make it easy to do business with us.

    RATE 1 2 3 4 5 ☐

IDEAS:
_____

I make it fun to do business with us.

    RATE 1 2 3 4 5 ☐

IDEAS:
_____

I set up the service with personal information --
I find their "why."   *RATE* 1 2 3 4 5 ☐

IDEAS:
_____

I discover things about my customer's
buying habits.   *RATE* 1 2 3 4 5 ☐

IDEAS:
_____

SELF-EVALUATION TEST
(1=poor, 2=average, 3=good, 4=very good, 5=the greatest)
(1=never, 2=rarely, 3=sometimes, 4=frequently, 5=always)

I ask about my customer's favorite things and
try to discover something that we have in   *RATE* 1 2 3 4 5 ☐
common or take an interest in them personally.
IDEAS:

I have ten solid lines that work when I'm
servicing customers -- they are posted by   *RATE* 1 2 3 4 5 ☐
my desk.
IDEAS:

I study new methods of serving.

    RATE 1 2 3 4 5 ☐

IDEAS:

When a customer says no, I know he's not
rejecting me -- only the offer I made him.   *RATE* 1 2 3 4 5 ☐
I don't take "no" or "rejection" personally.
IDEAS:

I use words of power and reassurance:
"Ms. Johnson, you made a great choice."   *RATE* 1 2 3 4 5 ☐

IDEAS:

I use angry calls as an opportunity to be the
most professional I can be and provide the   *RATE* 1 2 3 4 5 ☐
greatest service.
IDEAS:

I empathize with the customer's problem first.

    RATE 1 2 3 4 5 ☐

IDEAS:

SELF-EVALUATION TEST

(1=poor, 2=average, 3=good, 4=very good, 5=the greatest)
(1=never, 2=rarely, 3=sometimes, 4=frequently, 5=always)

I start with "YES." ("The best/easiest/fastest
way to handle that is...")   *RATE* 1 2 3 4 5 ☐

IDEAS:
_____

I recognize that people have other problems
that may increase their anger.   *RATE* 1 2 3 4 5 ☐

IDEAS:
_____

I know I can't win an argument with an angry
customer. So I don't argue.   *RATE* 1 2 3 4 5 ☐

IDEAS:
_____

I take away customer frustration by making it
easy for them to get the help they need.   *RATE* 1 2 3 4 5 ☐

IDEAS:
_____

I don't make excuses about why I can't.

                                              RATE 1 2 3 4 5 ☐

IDEAS:
_____

I avoid phrases of disappointment like
"We can't get anybody out there until..." or *RATE* 1 2 3 4 5 ☐
"We don't have any ___ right now..." or
"You should not have ___ ."

IDEAS:
_____

I know it's not just what I say, it's how I say it.
I always say it in a positive way.   *RATE* 1 2 3 4 5 ☐

IDEAS:
_____

SELF-EVALUATION TEST

(1=poor, 2=average, 3=good, 4=very good, 5=the greatest)
(1=never, 2=rarely, 3=sometimes, 4=frequently, 5=always)

I use the word "personally" in my talk when
I make a commitment. *RATE* 1 2 3 4 5 ☐

IDEAS:

I can quickly forget the last call if it was bad.
I can just put it out of my mind. *RATE* 1 2 3 4 5 ☐

IDEAS:

I call customers back after the problem. I call
back and ask if they were served okay, *RATE* 1 2 3 4 5 ☐
and that all is well. Then I sell more.

IDEAS:

I substitute the words "so we can be fair to
everyone" for the word "policy." *RATE* 1 2 3 4 5 ☐

IDEAS:

I stand up every once in a while when I'm
talking on the phone. *RATE* 1 2 3 4 5 ☐

IDEAS:

I record myself for 1 hour each week,
and then listen to it in the car. *RATE* 1 2 3 4 5 ☐

IDEAS:

I learn from my co-workers.

RATE 1 2 3 4 5 ☐

IDEAS:

SELF-EVALUATION TEST

(1=poor, 2=average, 3=good, 4=very good, 5=the greatest)
(1=never, 2=rarely, 3=sometimes, 4=frequently, 5=always)

I do my job with pride, because I'm proud
of who I am.   *RATE* 1 2 3 4 5 ☐

IDEAS:

I invest 20 minutes a day in learning
something new.   *RATE* 1 2 3 4 5 ☐

IDEAS:

I am the greatest -- because I try to be,
and think I am.   *RATE* 1 2 3 4 5 ☐

IDEAS:

I know it doesn't matter what I want --
it's what *customers* want. I strive for that. *RATE* 1 2 3 4 5 ☐

IDEAS:

I know it doesn't matter what I think, do,
or say. It only matters what *customers perceive.* *RATE* 1 2 3 4 5 ☐
I practice this principle.

IDEAS:

I thank customers for everything.

                                                RATE 1 2 3 4 5 ☐

IDEAS:

I say "THANKS" in some creative way every
time I end a call.   *RATE* 1 2 3 4 5 ☐

IDEAS:

12

Put Your Job Skills to the Test

SELF-EVALUATION TEST

(1=poor, 2=average, 3=good, 4=very good, 5=the greatest)
(1=never, 2=rarely, 3=sometimes, 4=frequently, 5=always)

I know I'm only responsible for one person:
Me. *RATE* 1 2 3 4 5 ☐

IDEAS:

I do everything I can to stop internal
negative talk. *RATE* 1 2 3 4 5 ☐

IDEAS:

I don't blame others or grumble about
my situation. *RATE* 1 2 3 4 5 ☐

IDEAS:

I resign my position as general manager of
the universe. *RATE* 1 2 3 4 5 ☐

IDEAS:

END OF TEST

GetReal...

How'd you do?
Not as perfect as you
thought you were when
you started the test?

JustTryThis...

Turn the page

OK,

now that you took
the test, what do you do
with the results?

Check the boxes (□)
to the right of the questions
where you scored a 1, 2, or 3.
Those are your weak areas.
Now meet with your boss --
yes, with your boss,
and establish a plan
to get better.

That's all there is to it --
except for dedicated hard work
for the most important
person in the world.

YOU!

Want a
daily report card?

WATCH, LOOK & LISTEN!

Watch for smiles --
when you get them,
you're on the right path!

Look for unsolicited letters
of thanks and praise --
when you get them,
you're on the right path!

Listen for "thanks" --
when you hear it,
you're on the right path!

and...

Listen for "WOW!" --
when you hear WOW!,
you're on *THE* path!

How

many

"memory"

chances

are

you

blowing

by

being

"ordinary"?

Answer:

Too many.

Lessons from the Real World

LESSONS I LEARNED SLEEPING IN SOMEONE ELSE'S BED

- All I wanted was an ironing board...
- "Sorry, no rooms tonight"
- Upping the standards and WOW!ing the customer
- A NIGHTMARE --
  Exceeding my expectations -- *Not!*
- A FANTASY --
  Creating plenty of room for error
- You can earn forgiveness BEFORE the error -- or not

How do ironing boards breed customer loyalty? Here's an example of an opportunity to gain loyalty and an opportunity missed:

ALL I WANTED WAS AN IRONING BOARD...

I checked in to the Drury Inn in Overland Park (a suburb of Kansas City). The staff was friendly.

As it was a "limited-service" facility, I dragged my own bags on a luggage cart to the front desk. The help the clerk offered was in the form of a question: "Can I help you with your bags?" I politely refused.

If he had helped me, I would have been "satisfied." BUT he had an opportunity to begin to breed loyalty by taking a memorable action. If the clerk had jumped from behind the desk and said, "Mr. Gitomer, let me show you to your room *personally*." (And with tongue in cheek said) "These halls are fraught with danger. Let me drag your bags down the hall for you, and ward off any lions or tigers that may gobble you up. We lost five guests who took their own bags down the hall last week. Pity."

I would have been howling with laughter and told everyone of the experience. Instead, I dragged my own luggage cart *satisfactorily* down the hall. He had a chance to take my bags memorably down the hall, but he blew it.

I got settled into my room and found no iron or ironing board. I called down to the front desk and asked, "Could you bring me an iron and a full-sized ironing board, please?"

Ten minutes later a nice guy bangs on my door and hands me an iron, and one of those mini-ironing boards for Barbie-doll clothing. "There are no full sized ironing boards," he said. "Sorry about that."

There I was -- satisfied again. Got the iron, kind of got the ironing board. BUT -- I hate those little boards. Ever try to use one? You can't iron anything on them. So, I call down to the front desk (again) and ask for a big people's ironing board. "There are no full-sized ironing boards," they said. "In the world, or just at this hotel?" I asked.

The front desk person didn't get it (surprise), so I decide to take my satisfaction into my own hands. I drive 4 miles down the road to Wal-Mart, and buy a big-people's ironing board (for $12.88).

Ever walk INTO a hotel with an ironing board under your arm? Let me tell you, you'll get a few looks.

Here's how the story ends: The general manager offered to pay me for the board -- I refuse the money and donate the ironing board to the hotel so that other salespeople with wrinkled clothing could get some use from it.

The story COULD have ended with a positive (loyalty breeding) spin, if the person at the front desk had been trained to start with YES. Instead of saying, "There are no ironing boards," he could have said, "The best way to handle that is..." or "The easiest way to get one is..." or "The fastest way to get one is..." and would have been forced to come up with a solution.

For thirteen bucks they could have been heroes instead of goats. The hotel person could have asked me, "Jeffrey, is a full-sized ironing board important to you?" "Yes," I would have replied. "Well, if you can wait fifteen minutes, I can make one appear." That's what I wanted to hear. How tough would that have been?

The biggest reason that positive endings don't happen is because employees are trained on policies and rules (why you can't do things), rather than principles (think "yes," and figure out how to deliver, even if it means leaving for a few minutes and spending a few bucks).

How many "memory" chances are you blowing by being "ordinary?" *Let me give you a few examples of missed every-day opportunities:*
- **Weak service offerings in the form of questions** -- "Will there be anything else?"
- **Dumb voice-mail message** -- "I'm either on my phone or away from my desk." Oh boy! There's an intellectual and spirited message if I ever heard one.
- **Boring fax cover sheets** -- Using the same old ragged edge piece you made up two years ago that detracts from your image.
- **Rude-sounding initial phone greeting** -- Spoken too fast for anyone to understand it, or said in a matter of fact tone.
- **Recalcitrant (monotone) receptionist greeting a visiting guest** -- "Your name is?" "You're here to see?" "Do you have an appointment?" "Can I tell him what this is in reference to?" Make me puke.

NOTE: These actions are NOT the fault of employees -- they're the fault of the person who trained them, and the person who decided the training content.

ACTION: What can you do? Start by identifying every action or contact with a customer, and change each one to a new, better, creative, memorable, loyalty-breeding action.

CHECK THIS OUT: At the end of my Drury Inn stay, I was handed an envelope as I checked out. It was a twenty-dollar bill and a coupon for a free night's stay. Very nice (lesson).

How were you trained?
Any different?
Were you trained to be ordinary?

Create "best" responses
for each ordinary action.
HOW you say it makes
all the difference.
And how.

Conrad Hilton creates a powerful "new" service.

"SORRY, NO ROOMS TONIGHT."

Presented here is one of the most powerful lessons of this book. It's from a man who was arguably the father of hotel hospitality... Conrad Hilton.

The story is from the book *The New Art of Selling*, by Elmer Letterman, published in 1957. The chapter is titled, "Ten Creative Sales and How They Were Made," but this is a story about providing service beyond the normal thought process. This is about the philosophy **"Just because we don't have anymore, doesn't mean the customer's need goes away."** Here is the story without an edit. (Obviously, it's taking place in the late 1940s.)

ONE MAN WHO CREATED A SALE BY CREATING A SERVICE. One of the most overworked words in salesmanship is "service." I would like to remove it from applying to those regular attentions which any sensible salesman gives to his customers. Service, to my mind, should mean a unique, new, tailor-made, extra contribution made to a customer's welfare beyond mere routine follow-through.

When Conrad Hilton took over the Palmer House in Chicago, all hotels were crowded in the wartime rush for accommodations. Travelers found themselves roomless and frustrated. Hilton saw day after day the familiar sign: "Sorry! No rooms today without reservations." It got on his nerves. That word "sorry!" stuck in his crop. It was weak, and it looked insincere. Suppose he were a traveler just arrived in the city looking for a room in the Palmer House? He could feel his own gorge rise.

It was not long before that sign was down. In place of it, he set up accommodation desks with hotel representatives at them ready to help a stranded traveler find a room in another hotel. They did not always succeed in their quest, but there was no doubt in the mind of the guest that the Palmer House sincerely wanted to help him. It stood the hotel in good stead when later days brought about a situation in which there were more rooms than guests.

A second source of irritation in those overcrowded days was the delay often experienced by a guest with a reservation who arrived only to be told that his room was occupied until 3:00 checking out time. Instead of leaving him stranded, Hilton set up facilities in the hotel where he could take a shower and shave immediately, and have any messages telephoned to him.

The hotel also stamped the reservation cards given to the delayed guests at the desk with various hours for returning to claim their rooms, 1:00, 2:00, thus staggering them and preventing long waiting lines at 3:00. Here was creative thinking of a high order.

The customer came for a definite product. In the nature of things, he could not be given that product. The problem presented, therefore, was to retain his good will while being unable to satisfy his specific demand. Hilton did this by a series of unique and ingenious new combinations of old ideas. There was nothing new about the idea of trying a second hotel when you couldn't get into the hotel of your choice.

There was something decidedly new, particularly in that period of competition, about one hotel going out of its way to find a room for a guest in another hotel. It gave a new dimension to the word "guest" as applied to the hotel business. What Hilton was virtually saying was this: "Any man who comes to the Palmer House first is, by that act, making himself our guest, and we will take care of him as an individual would take care of a guest at his house.

If we can't accommodate him, we'll get one of the neighbors to do it, and even when he stays in the neighbor's house, he will recognize that he is still our guest. He is our guest even though we are temporarily forced to put him in another hotel."

With the same ingenuity, he said to himself: "If a man comes with a reservation and can't get his room, he gets sore. From his point of view, he has a right to get sore, but why does he want that room at once? Because he wants to be able to get messages, and because he wants to attend to certain personal needs. I can't give him (all) the room he desires, but I can give him some room." This was a fresh look, and a solution which created a new service in the midst of the pressures of an extraordinarily harassed time.

> This example is all the more valuable because it carries none of the overtones of over-sentimentality which sometimes give a false note to talk about service. This was a new service created within the framework of the hotel business and having, definitely, a hotel flavor. Yet it went beyond the limitations of a mere institutional gesture. It combined personal attention with professional practice ingeniously.
>
> It was creative within the techniques of its own operation, a fact which took from it any air of artificiality, yet left an impression of sincere thoughtfulness.

Well, what can we learn from this? On one hand, you couldn't blame anybody who's a regular employee from saying, "We're sold out right now. We don't have any more. We're out of stock with that item right now." And, the customer says, "Oh, rats," and goes away.

But the other hand says, "FULFILL THE CUSTOMERS NEEDS, NO MATTER WHAT."

GetReal...My challenge to you is to take ownership of the problems that come your way. If you take ownership of the problem, then you take ownership of the customer. If you try to delight customers in every way (even when you think you can't), you will become a long-term winner. If you let them go away, someone else is sure to take care of them that day -- and for days beyond.

Problems often show up as opportunities in disguise -- it's all in how you view them. And the cool part is -- The choice is yours.

Just because you can't fill the need, does not mean the need goes away -- it just means someone else gets to fill it -- guess who?

JustTryThis...*The challenge for you is to think of what other ways you can respond or react other than saying, "We're sold out," or "We're out of stock," or "We don't carry that," or "We're not taking any more reservations," or "That sale ended yesterday."*

Here's the secret: just say it in a way that you would want to hear it. Just do it in a way that you would want it done to you. GOLDEN.

UPPING THE STANDARDS -- AND WOW!ING THE CUSTOMER.

"Hi, my name is Kim Waggy, I'm the concierge at the Broadview Hotel (in Wichita, KS). You'll be staying with us on the 15th and 16th of October, and I'm calling to see if you need anything special."

Oh my God. Total shock. Five hundred hotel stays over the last three years and this is a first in service. I screamed at our staff. Told them Kim's quote. They gave her a standing ovation on the spot. Over the phone I could hear Kim blushing. Memorable service is about surprising someone. I was flabbergasted.

I couldn't think of anything I wanted. So, I asked, "Well, what does everybody else ask for?" (Hoping for a few suggestions.)

I asked Kim what typical reactions were to her call. "Surprised, very surprised," she said. "People realize we're going an extra step to satisfy their needs. It makes the guest feel more welcome, helps people remember us as a step above. Pleased -- valued -- thought of. Not just a name in the computer."

I don't know about you, but I wanted to find out what people ask for when they get Kim's call. "Very little out of the ordinary. That's not the only reason we call them. We want our guests to have an experience here, not a stay -- and we believe that starts before the guest arrives. I make sure my friendliness and service orientation set the tone and the expectation for their stay." WOW!

"How surprised are they?" I asked.

"Well, today three people dropped the phone." she said.

For the curious, here are the top eight things they ask for. The most requested items when the concierge calls first:
1. Iron and ironing board.
2. Special food.
3. Electronic hookups.
4. Newspapers (like the *Business Journal*).
5. Refrigerator.
6. Juice, soda.
7. Places to eat.
8. Places to have fun.

"How did you come up with this idea?" I asked.

"Leo Villafana, our front desk manager, came up with the idea. We have a weekly meeting to review the guests coming in. We were brainstorming, trying to EXCEED their expectations. We were stuck for an idea about the best way to find out the guests' needs, and Leo said, 'Why don't we just call the guests and ask them?' (duh) We decided to call each guest one week in advance to pre-determine their needs. If we don't ask, we won't know. If we don't know, we can't wow." WOW!

"We just implemented this practice a few weeks ago. The response has been positive," said Kim with her Midwest modesty. "Most people don't need big stuff. But they love the call."

I asked to speak to Leo Villafana. There was great music on hold -- no surprise.

"Our corporate philosophy is to put the person staying at the hotel at the top of the list. To make customers feel special," Leo said. "Grand Heritage feels that every guest should be a name, not a room number. The advance call is not just a courtesy, it's a philosophy." Cool.

Stop for a second to consider what this hotel has done. The (competitive) advantages are staggering:

First: (and most important): they have created a shift from *reactive service* (the guest shows up and checks in), to *proactive service* (call the guest in anticipation of their arrival). *Which do you think is more powerful?*

Second: taking the concierge to the guest significantly reduces calls to the concierge desk during the guest's stay.

Third: repeat business. "We get lots of returns," Leo said. "Our guests come back."

Fourth: lots of people spread the word -- *for free*. Look at what can happen when you surprise someone, and they tell someone else. I hang up from Kim and tell someone else. Kim makes 25 calls a day. 125 calls a week. 500 calls a month. 6,000 calls a year.

A minimum of 6,000 happy, surprised guests telling 6,000 other potential guests. 12,000 if everyone only tells *one* other person. Small investment. Big reward. Wouldn't it be nice to have 12,000 ambassadors a year talking about your business? That's nothing. So far I've told 10,000 people and the readers of the 55 business journals. That would make over 1,500,000 ambassadors, and I've just started.

I asked Kim if there were any personal benefits from this new concept. "There's something about making others happy that makes your own problems seem small," said Kim Waggy. Well said.

My requests? Just my standard needs -- an iron and an ironing board that's not for Barbie Doll clothes. Plenty of plugs for computers and modems. But I had to challenge her -- I asked for a used bookstore -- specifically for used books on selling skills and personal development. She said -- "I'll have a list ready when you get here." Cool.

I figured the stay would be equally as wonderful. I was right!

The parent company, Grand Heritage Hotels, buys historical buildings and restores them to their original elegance and grandeur. When you walk in, the hotel makes its own statement before anyone says a word.

OK, I'm ready -- hit me in the service-plexus. The front desk greeting was standard. Rats. "Last name?" she queried. I wanted to say "Welcome," but I didn't dare. She handed me a pile of messages and stuff. Mail, I love mail.

I got to my room. Big. Clean. Fluffy towels. Big ones.

Then a series of way-cool things began to happen:
• Kim Waggy (concierge) had accepted my challenge to find used books on selling and personal development. Not only did she have a list of bookstores, she also had a list of books.
• The newspaper under my door the next morning was a *Wichita Business Journal*, opened to my article, and a note from the general manager, Larry Weber, saying how much he liked it (nothing beats a general manager with good judgment).
• I had a wake-up call from a real live human being telling me, "Good morning," and that it was 65 degrees outside.
• I had a torn vest -- they fixed it within two hours, and didn't charge me.

They did things that made me feel good -- no, they made me feel great.

I talked to the employees. Listen to these attitudes:
"I'm constantly trying to create happiness, constantly thinking of ways to be memorable. It's challenging, it's fun," said Kim Waggy, concierge. "I'll look up a reservation and see where someone is from and see if I can find the guest his hometown paper."

Leo Villafana, the front desk manager, defines his customer service role as "taking an additional step. The extra step. A lot of times they're surprised. But for us, it's standard procedure."

Leo's customer service objectives are to:
• make them feel important
• make them feel special
• make them feel cared for
• make them feel at home

Here are Leo's ten hotel service hallmarks:
1. Saying welcome with a smile.
2. Making nice -- being overtly friendly (making small talk about them).
3. Learning about guests at the front desk.
4. Saying "hello" when a staffer passes guests in the hall.
5. Using humor.
6. Calling the room after check-in to see if everything is all right (leaving a voice mail if they're out)
7. Taking guests where they want to go. We have a van -- and we use it. We shuttle guests anywhere and pick them up. (Half the hotels in America tell you they're only insured to take you to the airport -- *and they're lying.*)
8. Sending cards after the stay -- hand written.
9. Making a meal reservation -- then calling the restaurant again when the guest is away from the desk -- and asking the restaurant for special treatment.
10. Handling everyday help and requests as though my job and the future of the hotel depended on it.

Then there's general manager Larry Weber, who says, "I want the people who work here to be relaxed and have fun." (What a

Lessons I Learned Sleeping in Someone Else's Bed

13

concept.) As we walked down the hall, I saw the real measure of
Weber. As we were talking, Weber saw a room-service plate left
outside a room. Without hesitation, he picked up the plate. Real
leaders are willing to do any job they supervise. On that hallway
walk, Weber was general manager and general clean-up. It was
nice to see.

I asked him for a philosophy on management as it relates to customer service. "Easy," Weber said. "I empower people to make
decisions the way I would. When they face any situation with a
guest, I tell them to imagine what I would do in the same situation, and do that.

"The power of that transference gives the employee a chance to
think of a positive solution without worrying 'what will the boss
think.' It helps clarify and reassure their decision," said Weber.
"And it's working. Our next step is to reward their decision. We're
going to name the program *Creative Solution Service.*

"Here's an example," said Weber. "Last week a guest was flying in
for a wedding. He arrived late, only to discover that the affair was
more formal than he had planned for -- and he had no tie. The bellman without hesitation, took off his tie and gave it to the guest.
That's creative-on-the-spot thinking.

"Most people don't want to be in a hotel, but we can make them
want to come back here when they visit our city again. And if we are
exceptional -- we can get guests to tell others who might visit us."

GetReal...
What are you doing to get your customers to tell others about you?

JustTryThis...
*List three things that you do (actions that you take) that are
memorable enough to get your customers talking about you.
List three things you could change that would make your
ordinary actions memorable. Now take a page from Leo's great
ideas -- call ten of your customers and ask them if they've
ever talked about you and what they say.
Ask them WHY they told the story.*

Hotel Nightmare

THE SHERATON WESTPORT EXCEEDS MY EXPECTATIONS -- NOT!

I arrived in the city of St. Louis. My friend David Slan picked me up at the airport, and drove me over to the Sheraton Westport hotel. We got there about 9:30pm.

I walked up to the front desk. A woman behind the desk gave me a sort of stern look and said, "Last name?" I said, "Gitomer." She said, "Credit card." And I handed her my credit card. She handed me a piece of paper and said, "Sign here." Which I did.

A pretty unfriendly welcome, if I do say so myself. I leaned over the front desk and said, "I'm going to need a luggage cart to take my stuff up to my room." She looked at me and said, "Our policy is, you have to have a bellman to use a luggage cart."

I thought to myself, a luggage cart isn't that difficult to operate is it? I mean, don't you just pretty much pull them one way and then if you want to go the other way, you pull the other way? I imagined the headlines in the next day's paper: "Guest Operates Luggage Cart Backwards, Many People Are Killed." But, I went back to talk with my friend David, and waited for a bellman.

Ten minutes later, no bellman. Now I was a bit testy. I walked up to the front desk again. Miss Friendly was waiting on someone else. I interrupted and said, "Hey, I said I need a luggage cart."

Whereupon, she got up even higher on her haunches and screamed, "I told you our policy is that you have to have a bellman to use a luggage cart. One will be here in just a minute." A minute later a bellman appeared on the scene. As he was taking my bags over to the elevator on his vaunted luggage cart, he leaned toward me and whispered, "Don't worry. She's like that to everybody." And I just howled.

When I got to my room I was tired and all I wanted to do was iron my clothing for the next day, jump on the Internet for a few minutes and answer my e-mail, and go to sleep. I looked around the room -- no iron, no ironing board. Most full service hotels in America -- Marriott, Hyatt, and Radisson -- have irons and ironing boards, and so do most Sheratons. This one did not.

So, I called downstairs and, of course, I got Rasputin on the phone again and said, "Hey, I need an iron and an ironing board." Five minutes later someone came to my door with an iron and ironing board for either midgets or Barbie doll clothes. I called downstairs to Miss Friendly and said, "I'd like an ironing board for big people, please." She sent me up a big ironing board, finally, and I began to iron my clothes.

Then I looked for a data-port to plug in my modem and go on-line. No data-port. The phones were from the Alexander Graham Bell era and there was no way to plug or unplug anything. Once again I called the front desk. I promised her that this was my last call, but I did need to find out where the data-ports were. She said, "The rooms don't have data-ports. If you want one, you'll have to get one from engineering, and they don't open up until 6:15 tomorrow morning." (She hung up.)

All of this (from check-in to no modem) took place in less than thirty minutes. It was not 10:00 pm and I was thinking to myself, "How bad can this hotel get?" I looked around the room and noticed a note card on my pillow -- one of those personal hand-written thank you note cards -- and I thought, "Oh, a note card just for me."

I opened the envelope. Now I'm going to quote it to you, verbatim, as I read it aloud. (I'm looking at the card right now -- I saved it.):

"Dear Mr. Gitomer: Welcome to the Sheraton Westport Inn and the city of St. Louis. It is our sincere desire to exceed your expectations. We are all committed to providing the finest in accommodations and service. If I can be of any assistance to you, please feel free to contact me." And it was signed, *"Best Regards"* by the General Manager of the hotel!

I called the guy on the phone the next day (I decided not to disturb him at 9:30 at night at home) and I said, "Next time, please do not exceed my expectations, just meet them." I added, "By the way, when's the last time you stayed here at the Sheraton Westport Hotel?" And, he said, "Oh, I've never stayed here."

He would have never written that note if he had. I said, "Listen, why don't you check in at 9:30 tomorrow night with a bunch of bags, some wrinkled clothing, and try to get on the Internet and see what happens to you. Do that before you write your next note to a guest."

None of the stuff would have happened to me if the manager would had ever been a guest in his own hotel -- had he "been his own customer."

A Fantasy

CREATING PLENTY OF ROOM FOR ERROR.

Teresa and I were flying into Pittsburgh for our third stay at the Radisson Hotel in Monroeville, Pennsylvania. We'd been hired there to do some training and had made friends with everyone on the staff. To our surprise, we were greeted at the airport gate by Paul Phillips, the doorman, Paul was wearing a button that said, "Welcome, Jeffrey Gitomer," and it had my picture on it. Cool.

He was carrying a half a dozen yellow roses, which he gave to Teresa. Real cool. He had a little luggage cart with him so he could put all of our carry-on luggage on it and walk us down to the baggage claim. Real, real cool.

Paul Phillips is a wonderful man who loves his job because he loves people. We get down to baggage claim and he says, "Get your bags and meet me outside at the curb." Paul pulls up with the van, and I pull out with my bags.

It's a one hour ride out to the Radisson. We get inside the van and in the back seat is a cooler full of champagne and two dishes of strawberries. "Man, this is the greatest." We're all telling stories, laughing and having a good time. The hour ride seemed like a minute.

We walk in the hotel and the entire front desk staff is just chomping at the bit to tell us everything they possibly can, welcoming us to the Radisson, suggesting things for dinner, telling us where the Kinko's is, talking about how late the stores are still open, and tells us there is a mall right across the street, and making sure everything is just A-OK.

We get up to our room and there is a *USA Today* on the bed. They had taken my photo and using their computer changed the headline to read, "Jeffrey Gitomer Helps Radisson Monroeville Become the Number One Hotel in America" alongside my picture. It was the greatest. There was a pillowcase with my photograph on it and a little quote talking about how I'm number one.

A few minutes later the phone rings and they want to know if everything is okay in the room, "No, it's not OK -- it's GREAT!" I exclaimed. We go down and eat dinner and come back upstairs to "Internet" and go to sleep.

At 2:00am the air conditioning breaks and it starts to blow hot air. I wake up and say to myself, "Ah, no big deal, I'll just turn it off and I'll just tell them about it in the morning."

I wake up the next morning and want to check the hotel (TV) channel to see where our meeting was being held. I pushed the clicker for the television. Nothing happened. It was broken. I thought to myself, "Ah, no big deal. I'll just tell them later."

The Radisson staff was so nice to me that there was no way I could complain over trivial things. They had already built a loyalty factor in me that said, "It's no big deal. I'll just talk to somebody about it, and I know they will fix it. I have confidence that they will fix it and I'll still be fine."

Get Real...

Things that go wrong in any business are measured by the quality of the relationship that exists at the time that they go wrong. If the relationship is great, it's no big deal. If the relationship is non-existent, it becomes a huge deal. The molehill becomes a mountain.

Granted, at the Radisson I was a special guest -- BUT...

Go back and reread the story about my nightmare at the Sheraton Westport. Its just three pages before this. What do you think would have happened, what do you think I would have done if my air conditioner broke at the Sheraton Westport in the middle of the night? What do you think would have happened if my clicker had broken? I would have had a different reaction. It would have been a bigger deal -- maybe just the thing to push me over the edge of anger.

Here's the challenge. Everyone makes mistakes; every business has its problems. If you give great service, you will be forgiven for a mistake, or even a series of mistakes. If your service is bad to begin with, you eat the mistakes. *How do you set the tone for a mistake? How much room for error have you built into your business?*

"Welcome!"

The

rarest

spoken

word

in

business...

also

the

most

powerful.

LESSONS I LEARNED SHOPPING IN SOMEONE ELSE'S STORE

- Go Away!
- Re-sign your Greetings
- No shoes, no shirt, no service, no customers
- Bagel, bagel on the wall...
- You don't have to buy it, just try it on
  (*sizing up customer service*)

"GO AWAY!"

It never ceases to amaze me how unfriendly the first few seconds of arriving at any building or business is. Businesses seem to take delight in telling you to "go away!"

Look around the parking lot and you will see signs: "No Parking," "Don't Park Here," "Pick Up Only," "No Loitering," "Absolutely No Skateboarding." or my favorite: "Parking for (name of business) ONLY -- Violators will be towed at their own expense."

Then, walk to the door and it will say, "No Soliciting," or "No Shoes, No Shirt, No Service," or even "No Smoking" (which you can argue about, but "no" is still the prevalent word).

The average brisk retail business has 500-1,000 customers a day walk through their doors. The same business may have two "solicitors" a month walk through the doors -- and they IGNORE the no solicitors signs anyway.

So, WHY would you greet the 1,000 customers A DAY at your place of business with the words "no soliciting" instead of the word "WELCOME!"? It makes no sense.

The reason? People who own, run, or work for the business don't think like customers. It's as simple as that. They have meetings ad nauseam about satisfaction and service, and then defeat their own purpose by sending the wrong message from the first second the customer enters the door. Brilliant.

And those negative signs? I went to the hardware store to visit the sign department. They had 42 signs telling you what you couldn't do, and none that said "welcome" or "thank you." The closest thing they had to a positive sign was OPEN.

Every time I walk up to a business, I look for the sign that says, "Welcome." But most of the time, every business where I try to "vote-by-spending-my-money-there," greets me with some form of "no." Pathetic.

GetReal...*How are you greeting your customers? Any different? How many ways do you say "No" at your business? Can you find one sign with the word "Welcome" on it?*

JustTryThis...*Put up a big "Welcome" banner inside your business.*

RE-SIGN YOUR GREETINGS

In the parking lot...

Valued customers of *(your name)* are welcome to park here! If you're not a customer of *(your name)*, you're welcome to park someplace else!

At the front door...

Welcome!

(Solicitors are welcome to face the prospect of being asked to leave.)

NO SHOES, NO SHIRT, NO SERVICE, NO CUSTOMERS

"Don't buy anything here," is not a sign you'd see in a retail store -- or do you? Are you selling the customer yes with your signage or telling the customer no?

I went to the "New Big Village Restaurant" (in Charlotte) for breakfast. The front door sign struck me. It said "Welcome." I realized how rarely I see that sign.

I went into another (nameless -- but big national chain) restaurant in the same vicinity. The FIRST THING I see is a sign that says "Shirts and shoes must be worn to be served." OK, I can live with that. Then I get in the place and a sign at our table says "This booth reserved for two or more persons." So I look on the wall for some help -- no luck. "No Credit Cards" and "Pay Here" by the cash register. There's a handwritten sign "Absolutely no checks of any kind." Two more on the cigarette machine -- "Use at own risk" and "NO refunds given out." And no place like this would be complete without a "No Loitering" sign -- they had one. But the killer was a framed sign that said, "Firearms Not Permitted." Which is a good rule for a place that threatens and intimidates you. Evidently they want to be the only ones with pistols.

This is a restaurant where just reading the signs leads to indigestion. What happened to "welcome"? Pathetic, huh?

NOW IT'S YOUR TURN - What about your place of business says *Welcome* or *Thanks?*

* Are your signs encouraging or discouraging?
* What subliminal message are you sending to your employees and your customers?
* Are your signs *you oriented* or *customer oriented?* Here it is in a nutshell -- "OPEN" says it in terms of **you**, "WELCOME" says it in terms of the **customer**.

Are you getting customer and employee referrals? Or is your business a "one-time I don't care if I ever see you again," kind of place? Don't answer that challenge until you read the signs. Your signs.

Do you think the sign "shoplifters will be prosecuted" will stop a thief? No. But what do the words tell your customers and employees? How about "no loitering"? The loiterers are usually the ones who can't read. Do you think "no soliciting" has ever or will ever stop a salesperson? As a minor protest, I went out and purchased a "Solicitors Welcome" sign that is displayed big and bold on the front door of our offices.

Dr. Paul Homoly, world-renowned (retired) implant dentist, had a parking lot in the rear of his building. As you walked to the front on a footpath, there was a sign in the garden that said, "Hello and Welcome." Homoly was also one of the most successful and respected dentists in his field. Coincidence or attitude? You tell me.

Here's a few recommendations for making signs more sales oriented:
- Inspect every sign in your place of business.
- Take off all the "no" and "don't" messages.
- Reword offensive signs. Change them to *positive requests* with "please" and "thank you."
- Reword the "harsh rules." Try, "we would appreciate," or "to help serve you better," as lead-in lines.
- Have a welcome sign and mat at your front door.
- If you have a cash register, put a *thank you -- we appreciate your business* sign on it, or *Thanks for joining us, come again soon.*
- Make every sign in your business a *positive action* sign -- signs that say "Yes." Signs that make people smile or feel good about reading them.
- You could go wild at the front door and have a sign that says "We're glad to see you."
- Try to use signage that state rules in positive terms. Here's an example: "Welcome to Joanne's Diner. We appreciate your cooperation with the dress code as required by the health department. For your protection and the protection of other customers like you, it's important that you wear shoes and shirts. Thank you."

Do signs affect your business? YES! Signs...
- Set the tone for your employee's work atmosphere.
- Set the tone for a customer visit.
- Show customers you care (or don't care).
- Show customers you appreciate them and their business.
- Get customers to talk about you in a nice way.

JustTryThis...
Create big, bold graphic banners instead of signs. Make your signs an attraction that people talk about. Create a "You gotta see these signs" business, and people will visit just to see the banners.

JustTryThis...
Reword signs that are time worn. Instead of "OPEN," say "WELCOME, we're glad to see you." On the way out have a banner that says, "We hope we have earned the privilege of seeing and serving you again soon."

JustTryThis...
Many stores now have live greeters. People whose only job it is to say "Hello, welcome, happy to see you." The two best examples are Wal-Mart and Bloomingdale's department store. Two radically different retail establishments that share two common threads. Both realize the value of positive welcome and both are very successful.

Businesses that sell to other businesses can get more creative with their "welcomes." Many businesses that entertain prospects and customers now have LED programmable signs, computer banners, or little welcome bulletin boards for personalizing welcomes to visitors. Prospects and customers love to see their names up in lights. It sets a positive tone for the meeting (and sale).

When you call on a business, how do you want to be greeted? Are you greeted with a warm feeling that inspires you to do business with them? Or are you immediately encouraged to slam the door on your way out and say to yourself, "NO, I WOULD RATHER BE POOR AND GO WITHOUT FEEDING MY FAMILY than do business with these people."

Set the stage for smiles, warm feelings, and a "yes" attitude with your signage. Go around your business RIGHT NOW and perform a sign-ectomy. Remove all negative signs and make new ones. The result will be happier customers and happier employees -- which leads to a happier wallet.

As I paid my check at the "New Big Village," I got another surprise -- The sign on the cash register said, "Thank you for your business." The lady took my money, smiled, and thanked me again. It felt good. I'll be back.

Do your signs sell the customer "yes" or tell the customer "no"?

AUTHOR'S NOTE: These are three isolated experiences that happened to me personally. They are not to be taken as the way a company always does business.

BAGEL, BAGEL ON THE WALL: WHO'S THE FAIREST OF THEM ALL?

I love bagels! Nine years ago when I moved to Charlotte you couldn't find one, now they seem to be everywhere. New bagel shops on every corner. McBagels. I went into a gas station yesterday -- free bagels with a fillup. They're everywhere.

Soon, the war will heat up for bagel supremacy of Charlotte, meanwhile the field of competitors is settling in. The winner will be determined by how well their customers talk about them behind their backs -- word-of-mouth advertising. Here are three cases for you to judge for yourself.

Bagel 1: Teresa and I had just finished a long jog. I panted, "Let's stop at that new Einstein bagel place (on South Boulevard) before we go home. I think it just opened." I walked up to the entrance only to find a sign: "Open next Monday." Rats. Before I could turn away, a man jumped up from his seat in the window at the store, ran out to greet me and said, "If you're here for bagels, we don't have any today, but here's a coupon for two free bagels when we open up on Monday."

Wow, I wasn't expecting that. I was expecting, "Sorry, we're closed." I went back on Monday. The place was packed. The staff was friendly. The bagels were good, BUT no egg bagels, my favorite. I said, "Do you have any egg bagels?" "No," she said "But we've had lots of requests for them. Come back in two days, they'll be here." I did. They were.

Wow. I wasn't expecting that. I was expecting, "Sorry we don't have them yet." I bought 6 bagels, they gave me a 7th for free. Friendly people. Good bagels (the kind I wanted), and they gave me another coupon for a free bagel with cream cheese, if I came in before the end of the month. Double Wow.

Bagel 2: 7:56am, Saturday. I drive up to Manhattan Bagels (on Woodlawn Road) on my way to a meeting. A crowd of people stood outside of the door peering in the window. The sign on the door says 8:00am - noon. I tap on the glass. Someone looks up at me and lip-syncs "8 o-clock," in an act of defiance. The crowd grumbles. Five of the nine people decide to leave and go to Bruegger's.

Now it's 8am on the dot, my tapping on the window changes to banging on the window. "The last angry man" barges out the door as he opens it, obviously annoyed with having to open the store on time. I couldn't help but sarcastically say, "I apologize for wanting to buy something from your store so your children can eat tonight." Which he took as a negative.

Bagel man swore at me several times -- so much and so loud that Teresa my bagel-mate sitting in the car, locked the car door for fear that Bagel man might open fire. Inside the store, the cashier gave me five rude excuses in a row about how many wholesale account orders had to be filled that morning, and how the boss is too cheap to hire enough people, and how she offered to quit, and other assorted inane comments.

I got my bagels and escaped the store alive, vowing never to return. I made a mental note that they should stock an additional profit item -- bullet-proof vests.

Bagel 3: After another jog, I stopped at Bruegger's Bagels on More-head Street. I got to the front of the line and ordered an egg bagel. "We don't have egg bagels," she said triumphantly. "How come?" I said. "Egg bagels have too much cholesterol in them," she said, "We serve health-conscious bagels."

Really, I thought. They put enough cream cheese on their bagels that your arteries could harden by the time you got to the cash register if you took a bite. Why don't they just tell me, they don't feel like making egg bagels, or that egg bagels cost too much, or they decided not to make egg bagels. I could live with that. Why don't they just tell me the truth?

So I continued, "Just give me a plain bagel and toast it please." "We don't toast bagels," she said triumphantly. "Oh," I said. "Does any-one ever ask for toasted bagels?" "Sure, all the time," she said, "but we don't do it."

Think about that for a second. Here's a store that delivers a hypo-critical message about health to their customers, and has made a conscious decision to ignore the desire of their customers -- often. Good move. Seems like the right kind of attitude that will keep customers coming back. NOT! (NOTE: They got a toaster last week -- after two YEARS of ignoring customers.)

Bagel Report: I like bagels. I like toasted bagels. I like egg bagels. I like friendly people. Those being my desires, the field of bagel stores has narrowed to a precious few. And while the above three stores remain open for business, my big question would be -- for how long?

GetReal...

When competition stiffens, the only businesses that survive are the ones who offer the best value, friendly memorable service, and meet their customers needs. The same in your business. Think about that the next time you want your bagel toasted.

Think about that the next time you tell your customer no.

Are you in business to enforce your company policy or to serve your customer?

JustTryThis...

Make a list of the things your customer wants that you don't have. See what it would take to make one thing on the list happen.

Watch what happens when it does.

AUTHOR'S EPILOGUE: Bagel 2 closed their business last week. No surprise.

YOU DON'T HAVE TO BUY IT, JUST TRY IT ON.

(sizing up customer service)

"May I help you?"
"No thanks, just looking."

That's how retail sales are solicited in 75% of America's stores. Pathetic. So is the service that accompanies that pathos.

Do you remember the last time you had a really great experience in a retail store? Did you tell someone else the story? Remember the time you had horrible service? How many friends heard that story? People tend to repeat horror stories 5 times more than good ones.

Memorable customer service is the essence of building a business. Finding a customer is easier than keeping a customer. Getting a customer to return often depends on the quality of service delivered. Perceived service. After about 200 years of retail sales and serving the public, you'd think we'd have it wrapped. Air tight. Perfect service every time. We don't.

The stories below are not about what's wrong -- examples of that occur every day of our lives to one degree or another. This is about what's right! The rare examples of outstanding, memorable service that I hope will serve as a standard of excellence for *your* business.

Here are a few examples of "the right way" to perform service.

Clothing. I didn't like it at first. It didn't look like my style. "Just try it. You don't have to buy it." said Moustafa Saad, manager of Porta Bella -- a men's store in Manhattan with 5 locations.

I didn't really like it on the rack, and I resisted, but at Moustafa's insistence, I tried it. It looked good. In fact, it looked great. So, trying the last bastion of resistance I said, "I'm only in town two more days. How long will it take to alter the pants?"

"I'll do it for you right now," said Moustafa.

No way to get better service than *right now*, I thought. "I'll take it," I said.

Lessons I Learned Shopping in Someone Else's Store 14

Moustafa was just warming up. As I went back into the dressing room, he handed me another suit. "Just try it. You don't have to buy it," he said. "OK, OK," I said.

Meanwhile, I had fallen in love with a suit on the rack that was not my size -- and was searching size tags frantically. Moustafa, noticing my desire, was secretly calling the other four store locations to get the suit in my size while I was trying on my second suit. As I walked out of the dressing room -- in love with the (second) suit he made me try on, there was the (third) suit I liked -- in my size. I was speechless. And if I didn't quit buying soon, I'd also be penniless. But Moustafa had me in a buying mood.

After the fifth suit, I finally had to leave for an appointment. All five pairs of pants were completely altered. He gave me a discount for volume, and offered me an invitation to come back the next day to look at some new fall items he would get from the warehouse especially for me. I said OK. I was hooked. The lesson here is not just service, it's instant service combined with product knowledge.

Grocery Store. The other day I wrote a check at the grocery store. The cashier looked at my name on my check and said, "Hey Jeffrey, have yourself a good day." It felt great. It wasn't the standard phony "have a nice day," this cashier was into it. She meant it. She was having fun.

Restaurant. Two of my favorite eating places in Charlotte are Lupie's and Belle Acres Country Club. What makes them different? They combine great food with friendly people.

Since I eat out 1,000 times a year, when I go to a restaurant I want four things...
1. Great food.
2. Great service.
3. Friendly people.
4. Cleanliness.

It seems obvious to me that all restaurants would have this. Wrong again. It's so rare in fact, that less than one in one hundred places I eat meets this standard.

At Lupie's the food is as outstanding as the personal service. The first time I went in there, our waiter, KC, sat down at the table *with us* to take our order. Kind of like sitting around the kitchen table at home. He reinforced our choices, showed us how to save money by combining menu items, and was memorably friendly. He made us feel at home. I refer to the place as my "kitchen table." I eat there as often as I can.

Belle Acres Country Club is not a real country club in the truest sense of the word. Yes, it's a private membership club, but the golf course is a 9-hole putt-putt. The owners, Bud and Andrea Nachman, are there every day to serve their customers personally. They have combined a "theme" (sports memorabilia museum) with putt-putt, basketball, billiards, a great jukebox, superb food, and friendly people. Customers come there because they love it.

Belle Acres is a rare place. It has earned a rating of "great" in all categories: food, atmosphere, and friendliness. Belle Acres is memorable in every way.

One other thing that Lupie's and Belle Acres have in common -- they're both crowded. Surprise!

Hotel. I stayed at the Royalton Hotel last week. One of the most pleasurable hotel experiences of my 25-year travel career. How's this for service...
- There were two greeters outside the front door who attacked the taxi and had me and my bags out of the car in 30 seconds.
- Smiling doormen hold every door, and happily offer assistance. Immediately.
- They have a first class lobby -- clean and accommodating.
- Their men's room, with its unique plumbing fixtures, has become an in-house tourist attraction.
- All phones are answered within 2 rings.
- The concierge got me tickets to a show on the 4th row aisle -- at no extra charge.
- They deliver "extra" everything (towels, supplies, ice) within two minutes.
- Telephone messages are hand-delivered, slipped under the door.
- Fresh flowers are placed in every room every day.

- They provide a custom schedule of weekend events in the city for each room.
- Front desk people who smile, remember you, remember your name, ask how you're doing -- and mean it.
- Every single person is friendly and helpful.

What's so remarkable about this? The Royalton Hotel is a *positive oasis* in the heart of New York City -- the grumpy, get-out-of-my-way, I-know-everything, you're-an-idiot -- capital of the world.

The Royalton staff set the tone for my visit to NYC. They made me feel like a "King." They gave me a positive boost to go out and beat the city. Their prices are moderate for the city, but their service makes them the biggest bargain in New York.

Good Line. Said to me after I selected a shirt: "You made a great choice." -- *Chris Zeto, Bloomingdale's Department Store.*

Better Line. I was shopping for a new pair of running shoes, and in my mind I wanted this new style that looked great. It was the most expensive shoe in the store. The owner, Larry Frederick, a running expert, was waiting on me. He said, "These shoes are great, but they're not the best for your type of foot." He went on to recommend a less expensive model (almost 50% less) that he felt suited me better. He lost $70 but gained a customer for life -- by being honest.

Best Line. I was shopping in a mall in Dallas at a store called *Papillon - Men's Favorite Place*. It was 9:15pm. I wanted some of the men's ties that were on display, but was having a hard time choosing because the selection was so good. I realized that time was fleeting, and the manager, Massoud Mahboubian, probably wanted to go home to his family after a 12 hour day of serving picky people like me. "How late are you open?" I asked. "We're open as long as you are here, sir," was his reply. WOW!

Lessons I Learned Shopping in Someone Else's Store   14

GetReal...

Memorable service is the standard for the 90's. Are you measuring up? Would you be a return customer at your store?
Would you recommend your store to a friend?
Would you rate your customer service as something worth talking about?
If not, your competition is breathing a sigh of relief.

JustTryThis...

Substitute one new response for a trite one each week.
Substitute something WOW! for something boring.
Watch your customer's reaction.
And re-orders.

GET REAL
People complain all the time -- you get angry calls all the time. **It's no big deal.** Keep it in perspective. It's not brain cancer that's not operable -- it's not a terminal illness -- **it's just an angry customer.**

The biggest breakdown in communication that prevents you from SOLVING a problem -- which is why the customer called in the first place -- is that you take their anger PERSONALLY. **Big mistake.**

Take the problem seriously -- not their language or tone personally. Help them, solve their problem, get real with them, make them laugh, make them say WOW! **You can do it.**

JEFFREY GITOMER

15

15

LESSONS I LEARNED FLYING IN SOMEONE ELSE'S AIRPLANE

- Late Flight Delight.
  Happiness at 30,000 feet
- The "Get Real" and "Un-real" of airlines
- It was just an ordinary flight
  from Ft. Lauderdale
- The Three-Option Opportunity
- Trying to escape Boston with a smile.
  No luck

LATE FLIGHT DELIGHT. HAPPINESS AT 30,000 FEET.

The British Air flight from Budapest was delayed two hours -- fog in London. We're already locked in the plane on the runway. Trapped like rats. Usually I'm so mad I can't see straight. But today was different. The crew was not American -- it was British.

The cabin crew supervisor (in Britain the title is "Cabin Service Director") Tony Adams grabbed the microphone and said, "There's nothing we can do about the fog -- but we can eat!"

The crew was delightful. Serving everyone real food with fresh-brewed coffee and tea. Everyone was full and we finally take off. About an hour into the flight, Tony Adams, announces "A bit more bad news, I'm afraid -- It seems the fog has lifted, but the air traffic has backed things up another hour. For those of you making transfers -- don't worry too much -- this plane was supposed to take off for Sweden two minutes ago." The entire cabin laughed.

Five minutes later, Adams is on the loud speaker again. "To pass the time, we're going to have a contest. Guess the collective age of the cabin crew -- and win a prize. And there's an additional prize if you guess my age exactly." I was shocked and amused -- so were the rest of the 150+ passengers. Fun on the airlines -- imagine that! Everyone was talking -- having a good time. The crew came through the cabin collecting scraps of paper from the passengers with their calculated guesses. The winner was announced over the loud speaker. WOW! -- I was one of three winners who guessed Tony's age "spot on" -- 46. Cool. My prize was nice, but not as nice as the feeling.

"Are we strapped in and ready for landing, sir?" the delightful flight attendant asked jovially with her classic British accent. "It's about that time," she said happily. For the first time in 500 flights, I couldn't wait to get my belt on.

Tony comes on the microphone as we fly over London and says. "Below us is the House of Parliament where John Major is temporarily in power." The entire plane roared.

They took a negative (obstacle) 3-hour delay, and turned it into a positive (opportunity) by making everyone extra happy.

☞ The *good* part -- when you do something out of the ordinary -- is that it not only creates a memory, it sets a standard. It's an act that's tough to follow.

☞ The *better* part -- when you do something out of the ordinary -- is that it keeps you challenged to improve it each day.

☞ The *best* part -- when you do something out of the ordinary -- is that your competition is woefully lacking by comparison.

Lessons I Learned Flying in Someone Else's Airplane **15**

On another British Air flight, I'm getting ready to get off the plane -- waiting for the typical insincere, robotic message -- "Have a nice day, and thanks for flying _____ (plug in the airline's name)." Instead -- the lively first officer grabs the mike and says -- *"Welcome to Paris -- If you're here for a business meeting -- I hope it's a successful one. If your here on holiday -- I hope it's a happy one. If you're making a transfer -- I hope its a smooth one. And when you're flying again -- I hope it's a British Air one."*

The people on the plane started to applaud. An unbelievable moment in customer service -- the customer clapping for the vendor.

GetReal...
When's the last time your customers applauded you?

THE "GET REAL" AND "UN-REAL" OF AIRLINES.

If you're in the Airline business, you have a captive audience when customers (erroneously referred to as "passengers") are on the plane. You have a chance to make an impression. When customers "de-plane" they talk about their flight.

All airlines have announcements and safety instructions. Every customer is captive to those messages. I fly US Airways most of the time. Their announcements are professional -- aimed at people's safety. One big problem: no one listens. The flight attendants read from scripts that are not real -- it sounds plastic -- it's fake -- not one ounce of sincerity in any word they utter. People on the plane are talking to one another while the announcements are in process because they are presented in a non-compelling manner.

Flight attendants, gate agents, and pilots drone on like robots thinking that it's "professional," when in fact it's BORING, and if done often enough is downright annoying. Pilots drone on about how high they're flying. Flight attendants drone on about how to insert the metal end of the seat belt onto the other end -- duh.

Now let's look at another airline doing the same thing -- Southwest Airlines. The pilot comes on the loud speaker and says, "Everyone roll up your windows. We're going to be going really, really fast." Every passenger is laughing and listening. Now the flight attendant follows up with, "For those of you that haven't been in a car since 1955, this is a seat belt" -- howls of laughter, and EVERYONE is paying attention. Yes! It's REAL.

A note about safety -- ask US airways about this writing and they'll tell you that they're concerned for "passenger" safety (note: they fail -- or refuse -- to acknowledge people as "customers"). This is but another load of bull heaped on the customer. Do you think for a minute that Southwest Airlines wants their planes to crash? Of course not.

At the end of a recent Southwest flight, the after-landing "taxi" from the runway to the gate seemed like it took forever. The pilot came on and instead of the "professional" announcement of, "Everyone remain in your seats with your seat belt fastened..." he said, "I guess you folks have figured out how come Southwest Airline tickets are so cheap. We fly you half way there and drive the rest." People started to applaud -- happy customers.

GetReal...

Which airline gets talked about? Which is fun?
Which breeds repeat business?
Which breeds loyalty?

Southwest wants their customers to have fun when they fly.
And their safety message, laced with humor will be paid atten-
tion to 1,000 times more than the drone of US Airways (and
Delta, and United, and American). But the kicker is that the
customers of Southwest will leave the plane and tell A
MINIMUM of ten others about the fun they had.
What do you think they say about US Airways?

US Airways...Delta...American...United
• are stiff as a board
• annoy you with useless information
• sound fake and plastic
• are so boring that no one listens
• are building ZERO loyalty (other than frequent flyer miles)

Southwest Airlines...
• makes you happy to stand in line
• makes doing business with them a celebration
• makes doing business with them fun
• makes doing business with them something to talk about
  when you leave
• makes you want to do business with Southwest another day.
  WOW!

Lessons I Learned Flying in Someone Else's Airplane

15

IT WAS JUST AN ORDINARY FLIGHT FROM FT. LAUDERDALE.

"Welcome to First Class," said Captain Marty Bell.

Startled, I stopped what I was doing to listen. I've taken more than 250 flights in the last two years, and this is the first time I have ever seen the pilot mingle with the passengers before the flight. (*Passenger* is the airline's poorly chosen euphemism they substitute for the real word, "*customer*.")

Bell came by my seat and looked at my laptop computer. He said, "That's about all you need today isn't it? What are you writing about?"

"You." I said.

I told him my shock at his person-to-person contact. "I do it all the time," Bell said. "I talk to older folks, the handicapped, and kids first. The rest of the people see me and talk if they want to. A lot of people are scared to fly and want to see the captain. Heck, I'm scared," he quipped.

"You do this before every flight?" I asked. "Oh yeah. It sets the tone for a great flight," he said with the voice of experience.

He walked all the way to the back of the plane -- stopping three or four times along the way. I watched as he tried on a Mexican sombrero, and kibitzed with everyone. This guy was great. Answering questions, helping people with bags. The entire cabin was laughing and in a great mood.

He had completed his goal of setting the tone.

On the way back to the front of the plane he asked a small boy if he wanted to see the cockpit. The kid's eyes lit up as he followed Captain Bell into the inner sanctum. "Here, sit in my seat," the captain said.

The boy was glazed. "Wow!" was about all he could muster, but the impression Captain Bell made -- and the kindness he showed, will last for years.

The child's mother thanked Captain Bell profusely. He responded with the humility of John Wayne at the end of a movie after he'd single handedly won the west. Bell had won the hearts of his passengers -- in 5 minutes.

Now we're ready to take off. Somehow, I anticipate the announcements will take on an unusual flavor. *"Greetings ladies and gentlemen, boys and girls. Welcome to US Airways flight number 3231 to Charlotte and New York, LaGuardia. I noticed a lot of you were coming back from cruises and vacations -- welcome back. The weather up north is a bit colder than here..."* A warm, personalized message.

Along the way we were treated to the captain's personal geography *and* history lesson about the Kennedy Space Center, Disney World, the Daytona 500 which we passed over *while the race was in progress. (Cool!)* Jacksonville, Savannah, Paris Island, Hilton Head, and Charleston. Fun stuff about vacation areas, golf courses, and other friendly repartee. After what seemed like 15 minutes, the plane landed.

As is my tradition on my way out of an airplane, I wanted to thank the captain and crew for a safe flight. As many times as I fly, I still think it's kind of a modern miracle that you can be in Ft. Lauderdale, Florida at 12:45pm and land in Charlotte, North Carolina less than two hours later. I find that thanking the flight crew affirms the magic, and lets them know how much I appreciate them making my business possible to conduct.

I saw the captain leap out of the cockpit and de-plane first. He was standing there in the jetway waiting to personally say good-bye and thank everyone. WOW!

"I'm going to write about you." I said as I walked off of the plane. "Why?" he puzzled. "Because I had an exceptional customer experience and I want to tell others," I said.

Marty Bell didn't just command the airplane -- he commanded the respect of the customers inside.

Lessons I Learned Flying in Someone Else's Airplane

15

"Make sure you mention US Airways. Be sure to tell them about the company," he shouted as I walked up the jetway.

Captain Bell -- to everyone on the flight today, you were the company.

That's the story. But there's a much more powerful lesson attached to the story. The most powerful customer service lesson I've found. It's called the three-option opportunity.

THE THREE-OPTION OPPORTUNITY
The most powerful Customer Service lesson in the world

The Three-Option Opportunity "service leads to sales" lesson... There were 125 passengers (customers) on the plane. Many, if not most, will be asked the question, "How was your flight?"

That same type of question will be asked to customers who deal with *you* after a product has been delivered or a service has been provided. The question will create dialog. The type of dialog it creates is entirely up to you.

The story will be re-told to fellow workers, business associates, family members, and/or friends, about their experience with you. This presents a *three-option opportunity:*

1. To say something good about you and your business.

2. To say nothing about you and your business.

3. To say something bad about you and your business.

Let me share some possible responses.
Think of them in terms of how your customers would respond.

Example

1. "Jeffrey, how was your flight?"
   "The greatest. The pilot was great, incredible service --
   best flight I've been on in two years...(and on and on)."
   "Wow, what airline did you fly on?"

2. "Jeffrey, how was your flight?"
   "Well, OK nothing special." (end of conversation)

3. "Jeffrey, how was your flight?"
   "You wouldn't believe how rude the flight attendants were.
   Let me tell you about it...(and on and on)"
   "Really? That's horrible! What airline?"

Captain Marty Bell was smart enough to realize that
he set the tone for the entire flight with his positive
words and deeds in the first 5 minutes of his
encounter with his customers.

Do you?

GetReal...

Customers don't make up stories about your business -- it is you who create them. The customer simply retells them. How the story is told, and what the content is, is up to you.

When people ask for a referral. "Hey Jeffrey, you fly all the time. I'm going to Dallas -- what airlines should I fly?" Three options will occur. You will either get...
1. A referral -- US Airways is the greatest.
2. Nothing.
or 3. A reverse referral -- Anywhere BUT US Airways.

NOTE WELL. If the experience was good, the customer may not pro-actively say something, but if the experience was bad -- you can bet your last dollar they'll bring up the story in the first 5 minutes of a conversation -- depending on the severity of the displeasure -- sometimes in the first 5 seconds.

This lesson of customer service is the most valuable I can offer. First because it shows how one front-line person represents and speaks volumes for a multi-billion dollar company (certainly more powerful than a bunch of rhetorical ads on TV that are so plastic they should be accompanied by vomit bags). And second it creates a classic opportunity to examine how customers can make or break a business after a transaction has taken place. *The Three-Option Opportunity -- which option have you chosen?*

It is said that 80% of American business is done by word-of-mouth advertising. What's the word on you?

The 7.5 advantages of great service...
1. It's free. Costs little or nothing -- worth a fortune.
2. It builds goodwill.
3. It builds customer loyalty -- customers actually look forward to the next time they will deal with you. Happy to do business with you.
4. It creates memorable experiences that will be retold time after time.
5. It makes your customers salespeople for your business.
6. It leads to referred business.
7. It makes it harder for competitors to steal away customers -- even at a lower price.
7.5 It creates a clear distinction between two companies engaged in the same business.

TRYING TO ESCAPE BOSTON WITH A SMILE. NO LUCK.

I get to Boston's Logan Airport 2½ hours early for my 6:30pm flight. I run to the US Airways skycap and ask if there's an earlier plane to Charlotte. He says, "Yes 4:30, you'll have to check in at the ticket counter -- let me take your bags for you." -- Great!

I get to the line -- tip the skycap -- I'm next -- walk up to the counter and say to the woman, "I need to change my ticket for the next flight to Charlotte, please." WITHOUT LOOKING AT MY TICKET -- WHICH WAS IN A "FIRST CLASS" FOLDER, she asks with a snip, "Are you first class?" I just glare at her and say, "LOOK FOR YOUR-SELF -- I need help, the plane leaves in 30 minutes."

She then proceeds to give me some song-and-dance explanation about how she HAS to ask everyone because someone may not be first class and there's a long line, blah, blah, blah. I tell her I'm not interested in her life story, I just want to get to Charlotte. She gets all puffy, like I'm the jerk, and proceeds to give me a boarding pass for the 6:30pm flight. *SERVICE LESSON:* **Customers only want to resolve their problems -- not hear yours.**

"I SAID I WANTED TO BE ON THE 4:30 FLIGHT LADY." "Oh, I didn't hear you," she whined. "No, sweetie, YOU DIDN'T LISTEN!" I exclaimed in frustration. *SERVICE LESSON:* **Listening has nothing to do with hearing -- it has everything to do with paying attention.**

"I can't give you first class, it's full. I can only give you a coach seat," she said, almost happily. "But I'll put you on the standby list." Great. If anyone fails to show, I get the seat I want.

I get to the gate 10 minutes before scheduled departure. The plane is already boarding, and I ask the agent how many first-class passengers have boarded so far. He says without looking at me, "We won't know that for a while." (Every other airport in America they can count -- Boston seems to be without that capability.) "OK," I say in a nice way, "Can you show me where I am on the standby list?"

"We never show that list to customers," he cracks. I've seen that list at least 100 times in the past year, so evidently this guy thinks he's the entire airline. And he is -- at this moment the entire airline is being judged by this gate agent's performance. My temperature is now at 104 and rising.

Lessons I Learned Flying in Someone Else's Airplane

15

I tell him, "I'll just wait here." Two feet from his face, eyes glued to his forbidden screen. *SERVICE LESSON:* **Customers only want to hear one word "yes!" They get mad when you give excuses why you "can't."**

The other gate idiot makes two wrong announcements about stand-by's, then yet another (unfriendly) US Airways person comes over and triumphantly announces, "There are no more seats in first class." Rats.

As I board the plane, I see there are two empty seats in first class. I tell the flight attendant my plight. "Just wait here," she says "until everyone is on board." One seat gets taken. One still empty. It's now 4:35, and she says -- "Take the seat." I'm ecstatic. *LIFE LESSON:* **The best seats in the house are always available 5-minutes before the show starts no matter what the guy at the ticket office says.**

Now the gate buffoons come on the plane to "check the seat count," and spot me in first class. The door moron comes over and says, "What are you going to use for an upgrade?" (in a last ditch attempt to piss me off) "I'm Chairman's Preferred -- don't need an upgrade." He cowers back to the Head moron who comes over to my seat with a list. Asks me my name. Pretends like he's checking me off, says, "OK" and leaves.

The passenger in the seat next to me is laughing out loud. I explain that even though I spend one hundred grand a year on US Airways, I have to act like a jerk to get basic service. Pathetic. *SERVICE LESSON:* **When you make a mistake, be professional enough to apologize.**

EPILOGUE: I called several people at US Airways to gripe -- I finally got the HEAD of Boston Logan Airport US Airways operations to call me. He assured me that he would call me back "soon" to straighten this thing out, and get the people involved to apologize to me personally -- No call. I guess we each have our own definitions of soon. *SERVICE LESSON:* **When you make a commitment, take ownership enough to follow through.**

AUTHOR'S NOTE -- I fly a lot, and US Airways is my main carrier. There have been many joys and disappointments along the way. Even though this story is a slam on the service I received, I would also like to take a moment to thank those who have been wonderful to me. US Airways is not a bad airline -- it's just an inconsistent airline. Sometimes they're great -- sometimes they're horrible.

How could one company that's so good, be so bad? Easy answer: Employees who fail to realize that the customer is their food, people who don't care, people who don't train properly.

The purpose of this chapter is to point out that people in service positions have to focus on the customer's needs, and think about how what they say affects the customer's perception of the entire company. All the past "goodness" fades into the background when today's "bad" rears its (very) ugly head.

And maybe I could have been a better customer. Maybe they had a series of jerks all day and I was just the last on a pile.

I'm not trying to teach anyone at US Airways a "lesson." The people who did what they did to me in Boston are beyond lessons. They need to be removed from serving the front-line customer until they have been trained in superior service and friendliness.

Lessons I Learned Flying in Someone Else's Airplane

15

GetReal...

How well are the people on the front lines of your company trained? How consistent is their execution? How responsible are they? How fast do they respond? How friendly are they? When is the last time you provided them a lesson in listening? What are you doing about it?

Just a few questions to ponder, as your customers ponder where to make their next purchase.

JustTryThis...
Be friendly.

You

can't

kiss

a burnt

customer's

ass,

it's

too

late.

16

College education

prepares you

to play "Jeopardy:

and

"Trivial Pursuit."

The rest

of what you need

to learn

about your success

you have

to learn

on your own.

JEFFREY GITOMER

LESSONS YOU NEVER LEARNED IN SCHOOL

(ARE THE ONES YOU NEED TO SUCCEED)

- The Great Jim Rohn says...
- Positive attitude is everything -- how's yours? -- **SELF TEST**
- Could the Problem Be You? *Take the "YOU"* **SELF TEST** *and Find Out!*
- Good, better, best. *Which one are you?*
- Post-it Note Goals -- A Miracle of Achievement
- What does the local news have to do with great customer service? *NOTHING!*
- Don't worry, college will prepare you for the real world -- *The difference between earning a living and earning a fortune*
- The winds. The tides. The career. They all change
- 10.5 ways to adapt change and incorporate it naturally in your life, and your life's work
- I wanna be a success! I wanna be a success! -- **SELF TEST**
- 12.5 Principles of life-long learning -- **SELF TEST**
- Three principles that lead to success and wealth

Most people won't do the hard work it takes to make success easy.

Jeffrey Gitomer

...
This section is about success...
your success.

JustTryThis...
Read it and act on it.

A personal challenge
from the
Great Jim Rohn:

*"Formal education
will earn you a living.*

*Self-education
will earn you a fortune.*

*You determine
how much of a fortune
you will earn by how much
self-education you
decide to get."*

WOW!

The Big Secret...

Quality performance (and quality service) starts with a positive attitude!

A POSITIVE ATTITUDE...

(the way you dedicate yourself to the way you think and act)
is your ability to think, listen, speak, and react in a purely positive way.

- To see the good in things... not the bad; to see how to make bad things good.

- To see the opportunity when an obstacle faces you.

- To see things from the *what is right* side... not the *what is wrong* side.

- To treat others the way you want to be treated.

- To encourage others when they need support.

- To forgive others who have hurt or offended you.

- To never let the negative things of the world effect/affect you for more than 5 minutes.

- To (almost) never have a bad day.

- To have something nice or humorous to say.

- To be internally happy.

- To work at maintaining your attitude every day.

When you can add to the end of each sentence...

"all the time"

you've got a positive attitude.

MISSING TWO-FOOTERS?

In 1960, at age 12, I met a college basketball coach on the court, and asked him for his best, niftiest pointer. He took the ball, walked under the basket, and shot an easy lay-up. "See that shot," he said gruffly, "99% of all basketball games are won with that shot, don't miss it," and he walked away. I felt cheated that day, but 20 years later I realized it was the best sales lesson I ever got. Concentrate on the fundamentals, 99% of all success is achieved that way.

The science of serving and selling has nothing to do with nuclear physics or brain surgery. It's about asking questions; helping others; believing in yourself, your product, your company; establishing long-term relationships; and -- having fun. It's all fundamentals. You don't need to be a professional ball player -- you just need to know how to shoot lay-ups -- *and not miss them.*

I received a fax from a Richard Thompson in Ohio. He said, "Thanks for the article on basics and attitude. My son's basketball team lost last night by missing two-footers. I'm sure I have lost sales and customers by missing easy, basic shots."

Get Real...

How many two-footers are you missing
because you're not concentrating on
the fundamentals of the game?
How many service (sales) games are you losing?
How are you serving others in a positive way?

JustTryThis...

Prove it to yourself...
take the positive attitude test
on the next two pages!

ATTITUDE TEST

Do you have a positive attitude?
Everyone will say yes, but you can prove it to yourself.
All you have to do is pass this simple 2-part test.

How to take this test...

Carefully. Circle the number on the right that most closely
represents your present skill level or present situation.

How positive is *your* attitude?

PART ONE

(1=all the time/daily, 2=frequently, 3=sometimes, 4=rarely, 5=never)

- I watch the news.   1 2 3 4 5 ☐
- I talk about the news.   1 2 3 4 5 ☐
- I am affected by or talk about bad weather.   1 2 3 4 5 ☐
- I am mad at someone for more than 1-hour.   1 2 3 4 5 ☐
- When something goes wrong, I blame others.   1 2 3 4 5 ☐
- When something goes wrong, I dwell
  on self-blame.   1 2 3 4 5 ☐
- I bring my problems to work.   1 2 3 4 5 ☐
- I talk about my problems at work.   1 2 3 4 5 ☐
- I take my work problems home.   1 2 3 4 5 ☐

PART TWO

(1=poor, 2=average, 3=good, 4=very good, 5=the greatest)

- I am an enthusiastic person.   1 2 3 4 5 ☐
- I am happy on the inside.   1 2 3 4 5 ☐
- I look for the good in things.   1 2 3 4 5 ☐
- I usually talk about the good in things.   1 2 3 4 5 ☐
- I say why I like things and people,
  not why I don't.   1 2 3 4 5 ☐

ATTITUDE TEST

PART TWO *continued*

(1=poor, 2=average, 3=good, 4=very good, 5=the greatest)

- I look for the opportunity when something bad happens.   1 2 3 4 5 ☐

- I forgive people who have hurt or offended me.   1 2 3 4 5 ☐

- If I have nothing nice to say, I say nothing.   1 2 3 4 5 ☐

- I often encourage myself.   1 2 3 4 5 ☐

- I use positive attitude language -- ("half full" or "partly sunny") I avoid can't and won't.   1 2 3 4 5 ☐

- I have a positive self-image.   1 2 3 4 5 ☐

- I exercise choices that build my attitude.   1 2 3 4 5 ☐

- I help others without expectation or measuring.   1 2 3 4 5 ☐

- I am more motivated to help people than I am to make money.   1 2 3 4 5 ☐

- I often encourage others to succeed.   1 2 3 4 5 ☐

- I am happy about myself and my life.   1 2 3 4 5 ☐

- I work on my attitude every day.   1 2 3 4 5 ☐

- I listen to attitude audio tapes, and attend seminars.   1 2 3 4 5 ☐

- I ignore people who tell me "you can't" or try to discourage me.   1 2 3 4 5 ☐

- I count my blessings every day.   1 2 3 4 5 ☐

- I believe in myself.   1 2 3 4 5 ☐

ATTITUDE SCORECARD

Count the number of 1's, 2's, 3's, 4's, and 5's
from the previous pages.
Enter them in the blank line by the number that matches.
Multiply each line and add the total
(example if you circled number 4 eight times, enter "8"
on the "4 X" line and a score of 32 after the = sign).

1X_____ = _____
2X_____ = _____
3X_____ = _____
4X_____ = _____
5X_____ = _____
Total Score _____

How Positive Is Your Attitude?

135-150 You've got a positive attitude! You are the greatest --
because you think you are.

120-134 You've got a good attitude and probably understand
what it takes to improve it. Go for the gold.

75-119 You're in the *big club* of people who think they have
a positive attitude, but don't. You're in need of skill-building help,
and must actively work on attitude exercises -- Every Day. The
side benefits of these exercises are that people will be attracted
to you and you will be happier than ever before in your life.

50-74 You've got a negative attitude and should read several
books on the subject. You will need to change some of your work
and personal habits as part of your skill-building sessions.

29-49 You've got to work twice as hard as the group above.

How to personalize the test

There are 30 total questions. *Go back and take any question you
scored 1, 2, or 3 and check the box to the right of it.* Those are your
weak attitude areas. The checked boxes become your personalized
game plan to get a more positive attitude. Now all you have to do
is take daily positive action.

Lessons You Never Learned in School 16

THE DAILY DOSE OF ATTITUDE
Take any of these books and read two or three pages a day.

Here are a few books and tapes that I believe will have a
positive impact on your success... Start with them and build
your library from there!

Book List...
• The Holy Bible
• Think and Grow Rich -- *Napoleon Hill*
  (*tape series also available from Nightingale and Conant*)
• Napoleon Hill's Keys to Success -- *Napoleon Hill*
• How to Win Friends and Influence People -- *Dale Carnegie*
• The Power of Positive Thinking, The Positive Principle Today,
  Enthusiasm Makes the Difference -- *Norman Vincent Peale*
• Success Through a Positive Mental Attitude --
  Napoleon Hill and W. Clement Stone
• The Greatest Salesman in the World -- *Og Mandino*
• Swim with the Sharks -- *Harvey Mackay*
• The Richest Man in Babylon -- *George Clason*
• As a Man Thinketh -- *James Allen*
• Seven Habits of Highly Effective People -- *Stephen Covey*
• Psycho-Cybernetics -- *Maxwell Maltz*
• Getting Past OK -- *Richard Brodie*
•Thinkertoys -- *Michael Michalko*
•The Sales Bible -- *Jeffrey Gitomer (Hey, that's me!)*

> *People who write about how you can, not why you can't.*

Tape List...
• Jim Rohn -- *The Art of Exceptional Living*
• Wayne Dyer -- *Pull Your Own Strings*
• Earl Nightingale -- *Direct Line*
  (*the best -- hardest-to-get -- set of tapes in the world*)
• Earl Nightingale -- *The Strangest Secret*
• Glenn W. Turner -- *Any tape he ever made*
• Denis Waitley -- *Psychology of Winning*

> *People who talk about how you can, not why you can't.*

Could the Problem Be You?

RATE YOUR YOU AND FIND OUT!

*Here are 11.5 things that make "you" strong enough
to be a great person. Rate yourself in each category from
one (poor) to ten (the greatest) -- and
see how great "you" are. Put your rating in the box.*

1. **Your image.** *How you look affects the way you are perceived. How do you look?*

2. **Your ability to speak.** *Your ability to convey the message. Are you a member of Toastmasters?*

3. **Your ability to establish rapport.** *Making the customer feel at ease, and developing some common ground as a basis for moving forward. Do you make the scene warm?*

4. **Your attitude.** *Your enthusiasm combined with your state of internal happiness. Not what you say, but how you say it. Are you positive plus?*

5. **Your product knowledge.** *Your convinceability. Do you know it cold?*

6. **Your desire to help.** *Desire to help shows through; so does greed. Does your help side outweigh your greed side?*

7. **Your preparedness.** *A confidence builder if you are, or destroyer if you aren't. Do you prepare for every customer?*

8. **Your humor.** *Nothing builds good feelings like good humor and a good laugh. Can you make others laugh?*

9. **Your sincerity.** *Shows through either way. Are you genuine?*

☐ 10. **Your creativity** (or your ability to create a memorable experience). *Can you generate customer loyalty by being different from the rest -- or are you still belly-aching that the customer is a pain in the butt, and other lame excuses that boil down to -- you couldn't satisfy the customer's needs. How creative are you?*

☐ 11. **Your reputation** (or the reputation that precedes you). *If you are well known in the community, or in your field, you may have an advantage. How's your reputation?*

☐ 11.5 **Your glue.** *The way you handle your total package. Your stature. The way you carry yourself. The way you put it all together. Your character is what leads to the credibility of what you sell and how you serve. How well are you "put together"?*

HOW'S YOUR YOU? *How'd you score? Perfect score is 120.*

If you scored from 110-120, you are a great *you* with a great success story to tell, and are setting a great example for others. 100-109: Pretty darn good you. *Climbing the ladder, and making daily progress.*

70-99: You ain't as hot as you think. *You're in need of a 20-minute personal daily workout.*

50-69: You're mediocre at service, and so is your success to date. *You have a decision to make. Stay and get better every day, or get out before you're fired, and blame someone else for all that's wrong with you.*

30-49: You stink. *Go to the nearest bookstore, buy Dale Carnegie's* How to Win Friends and Influence People. *Don't leave home until you read it.*

Get Real...

Making *you* great is fun. And it will make you a better server of others. *Oh, and for those of you who have a long way to go, here's the best advice I've ever heard to start (and stay) on the path to being the best:* **To become the greatest, you must first think you are.**

GOOD, BETTER, BEST. WHICH ONE ARE YOU?

Are you the best at what you do? Everyone wants success, but very few achieve the success they dream about. I'm on my journey just like you. In the process of studying, I came to a realization about personal achievement.

"Going for the gold" is wrong. *Being the best you can be* in order to earn the gold, or get the gold is a surer path to success. What path are you on?

Personal achievement. Success. Fulfillment. Big words that every person seeks. "Get there by setting goals," they say. "Wrong," I say.

Now, I'm not saying don't set goals. I *am* saying don't set big goals and think that they're the direct path to personal achievement, fulfillment, or success. They're not.

In my experience, I have found most people set their goals for the wrong things and reasons. The problem with "big goals" is that they are usually "big dreams." And to further complicate the goal process -- most goals are about "it" or "things," (material stuff like -- big house, long vacation, million dollars, luxury car -- the usual), not goals about "you," (personal achievement stuff like -- college degree, promotion, physical fitness).

Most people with big material goals end up at low achievement, low esteem, frustrated, and cynical -- or they just become complacent and accept their lot as mediocre. Why? And more to the point -- what's to ensure it won't happen to you?

I'm sharing a personal achievement (secret) formula I accidentally uncovered. Discovering the formula was an accident -- but there are very few accidentally fulfilled people. Success, achievement, and fulfillment are on-purpose. The principles successful people execute and live by are the basis (foundation) for their success. I'm presenting the elements I discovered so that you may compare them to ones you execute on your own journey.

Why are some people able to achieve their goals and others not? Big question. Is there a formula to follow? I can't tell you what will work for sure -- there's no universal law of achievement, no universal law of success. If there was, everyone would be successful.

It's most interesting to me that the people who make "big money" their ultimate goal, rarely attain it -- while those who make "being the best at what they do" or who "love what they do," almost always attain financial security. Why? They execute the *elements* of personal achievement.

There are elements of success, and degrees of achievement of success, tempered and limited by an individual's desire, determination, dedication, and drive. It's a combination of your persistence (never quit) and your positive attitude (I will get it because I believe I will, and I deserve it).

The other day on a radio interview, someone asked me if I had a success secret. "Jeffrey, how did you get to this position in sales? What drives you? Do you have a secret success formula?"

The question caught me off guard. Hadn't much thought about my formula. Didn't think I had one. I do have a philosophy, and I live my philosophy. Should I answer with that? No. That's not a secret. So, I answered with one simple truth that I live by -- *be the best*.

"When I found out I liked sales, I made one goal -- *be the best*." I said.

"When I discovered I liked writing, I made one goal -- *be the best*. When writing led me to speaking and training, I made one goal -- *be the best*. Last year I began to make sales tapes -- same goal, *be the best*."

When I got off the radio show, I rushed to my laptop to capture the essence of what I'd said. As I developed the thought, I realized that there was an *elemental process* -- a formula for personal achievement -- *best* is just one element in the formula. And I figured I'd add the word "secret" to the formula so that it was more likely to be read. No one likes a formula -- but a *secret* formula -- now you've got something.

So, there are six parts (elements) to the secret of personal achievement:
1. Vision
2. Love
3. Best
4. Attitude
5. Personal
6. Student

Best. The operative element of the secret is *best*. But it's not the first element, best is element number three. If you find something to do that you *love*, (the second element) and consistently strive to do your best, and be your best, -- all the goals about cars, vacations, houses, and the ever popular money, will appear. The material things are a *by-product* of personal achievement. They are automatically attached to *best*. So the question is -- what drives you to want to become the "best" at something?

Vision. The first element of the secret to personal (goal) achievement is to identify a *vision* and put it in front of your goals. Got a big goal? Sure you do, everyone does. The big question is -- What's before (in front of) your goal? Do you have a *personal vision* that will drive you to achieve all your goals? Where do you see yourself?

Love. Last year I made an accidental discovery. It occurred when I examined all the elements of my career and tried to structure some of my thoughts into a ten-year plan. I was asking myself "What do I do best? What do I love to do? Where have I been most successful? How do I want to spend the next ten years?" From those answers, I decided my success would focus around selling and customer service -- writing, speaking, and making tapes. I love selling and the selling process, and serving is an extension of selling.

Once I realized that my choices were also my passion -- the vision became clear. Having a *personal vision, loving what you do,* and *striving to be your best* are at the core, but unless you couple it with a *personal vision* to see the big picture and a love of what you do, you will never achieve best.

The rest of the elements are:

Attitude. Many people cheat themselves out of achievement and success by having the wrong *attitude* (element four). Ever hear anyone say, "They don't pay me enough to..." Ever think it or say it yourself? Those are six words that will keep you mediocre. Don't make the mistake of failing to be your best or do your best because someone isn't paying you. Who are you cheating? Achievement is not about *money* -- achievement is about *best.* If you don't think they pay you enough, ask yourself what you're worth.

Having the right *attitude* about money will make it happen faster than wanting lots of it.

Personal. So much has been written about goals that it has caused those dedicated to personal achievement to moan at the thought of another seminar on "Goal Setting and Achievement." It's not a matter of goals or no goals. Goals are a prerequisite for success -- the question is what kind of goals? The secret of goals is to make them *personal* (element five) not *material.* Make goals about *you,* not about *it.*

Which is a more powerful driving force -- to make your monthly quota, or be the *best* at sales? If you goal yourself to *be the best* -- the quota automatically is achieved.

The other aspect of *personal* is based on athletics. Athletes are always striving to achieve personal best. Not to beat everyone else (although that's a great accomplishment), just to beat their previous personal best. That keeps them going. It can keep you going too.

Student. I got clear vision in a Jim Rohn seminar. He said, "Whatever you want, study it first. If you want to be a doctor, study medicine; if you want to be a success, hang around successful people and study success." Rohn says, "Be a *student* (element six) first. And always be a student. Not just a father, a student father. Not a teacher, a student teacher." Wow, what a powerful piece of advice.

From the day I learned my first sales technique (January, 1972) I wanted to be the best at sales. I've been studying sales for 25 years.

That's why it's working for me. **I'm not saying that's how it works. I am saying that's how it works for me.** Follow the advice of Jim Rohn -- be a student first. With all my heart, that's how I believe it will work for you.

In the seminars I do, the best audience comment I get is, "Jeffrey loves what he does, and it shows." If you love what you do, people will say *it's in your blood.* And that blood-of-toil begins to manifest itself in your bank account.

Get Real...

Last week I was watching the musician Kenny G being interviewed on CNN. They asked him what drove him to his phenomenal success. He said, "I never wished for fame and fortune. When I found out I liked to play the saxophone, I just wanted to be the best. The rest just showed up." Cool.

And the real cool part is --
if you think that being your best
and doing your best
is just a bunch of baloney --
don't worry,
this information doesn't apply to you.
It only applies to those
who will pass you.

Lessons You Never Learned in School **16**

JustTryThis...

The shortest goal lesson of your life...

Post your goals (in front of your face)
on your bathroom mirror, and say
them twice a day.

Once achieved,
post your accomplishments
on your bedroom mirror
so you can start each day by
looking at your success!

Wow!

(Looking at your past successes
reinforces your ability to achieve
your present goals.)

What's the best way to achieve your goals?

POST-IT NOTE GOALS!

- Goals are the road map to success. *Everyone knows that, but fewer than 5% of our society sets and achieves them.*
- Goals are related to everything we strive to achieve from our daily to-do list to earning a million dollars.
- Goal setting and goal achievement is a science and self-discipline that must be practiced everyday. *How do you set and achieve your goals?*

How can a pad of Post-it notes put you on the path to greater achievement? *Follow the formula...*

1. **Write down big ones** -- On 3x3 yellow Post-it notes, write down your prime goals in short phrases with bold letters. (get $25,000 funding for business; New Client -- NationsBank).
2. **Write down small ones** -- Write down your 3 secondary goals in short phrases with bold letters. (read book - Dale Carnegie; organize desk; build new closet).
3. **Post them on your bathroom mirror where you can see them twice a day** -- You are forced to look at them every morning and evening.
4. **Keep looking and reading out loud until you act** -- You will look at them twice every day. You will read them aloud twice a day. You will look at them and read them until you are sick of looking at them, and reading them -- and then you will begin to accomplish them. By posting the goal in the bathroom you are consciously reminded of your goals several times a day. From there your subconscious gets into the act. Gnawing away at your inner soul until you are driven to take positive action. *Achievement actions.*

   At last you can say the magic words...scream them -- **I DID IT!**
   (Screaming positive things always feels wonderful.)
5. **Start your day by looking at your successes** -- After your goal is achieved -- take it off the bathroom mirror and triumphantly post it on your bedroom mirror so you can see your success every time you look in that mirror. Not only does it feel great, but you get to set the tone for a successful day every day first thing in the morning. Plus -- it gets you motivated to keep achieving more.

The program is simple.

The program works.

The results will change your attitude.
The results will change your outlook
about your capability of
success achievement.

The results
will change your life.

I urge you to give this process
a solid thirty-day trial.
Use more small goals than big goals at first,
so you can get immediate gratification.

Post it. *Post haste.*

WHAT DOES THE LOCAL NEWS HAVE TO DO WITH SUCCESS? NOTHING!

Watching the local news -- *there's* a great use of your time. Thirty to sixty minutes a day of useless information -- presented in 100% problem format. *"If it bleeds, it leads,"* That's the local news philosophy of presenting information. How does that affect your success? In the worst ways possible.

No one cares that Billy got all A's on his report card, or Mary earned her Girl Scout badge. Good news doesn't sell, therefore it's omitted. Rather what you get is distorted, negative information about two to three percent of the people affecting those who view it in the worst way possible.

(**NOTE WELL:** I am NOT saying don't watch [or read] business news. Information that can impact your industry or your customer should be watched and read intently.)

What does watching the local news have to do with serving? Negative nothing. (What?)

Serving is *solution* based -- the local news is *problem* based. If you watch an hour of problems every day for years, you become problem oriented. Then you drag the news-crap to work, and begin to negatively affect others with your pukey stories. *Hey did you hear what happened on the news...?* (barf) The news sickness is contagious. You get it by watching, and then infect others by telling them about it.

Do you think local news adds or detracts from your serving skills?

"Hey, Jeffrey," you say, "the news is the most popular show on television." It's popular because most of the people watching it lack direction or focus, or are miserable and looking for something or someone more miserable than they are -- I guess to make them feel better.

Need to know the weather? -- Poke your head outside in the morning. It's a lot more accurate than the weather guy.

Think the local news is so important? Got to watch it every day to keep up? What happened last Tuesday? What happened yesterday? *Same crap -- different day.*

Think the local news is worthy of your time? How many of you can look in the mirror and say, "I'm successful today, I'm where I am today, because I watched the local news." See what I mean? (By the way the same goes for Roseanne and Cheers -- eh, but not Seinfeld -- Seinfeld is funny.)

Here's a wake up call (if you're still not convinced). Let's say you've been watching the news for just a half hour a day -- for the last year. That's 7.5 full 24-hour days you spent watching problems. In 5 years -- that's 38 full 24-hour days. In terms of 40 hour work-weeks that's 23 weeks every five years -- and that's *only* if you watch the 6pm crap. If you tune in for more crap at 11 -- double it! *That's the equivalent of 46 forty-hour weeks of work.*

Imagine the possibilities if you diverted that energy in a positive direction. Imagine what you could do with that time, accomplish in that time, if you put it to productive use for yourself. WOW! (By the way, you don't want to know the twenty-year figure -- it's too scary.)

Which do you think is a more powerful use of your time: watching other people's problems, or investing in yourself and creating plans and solutions?

Here are 4 solution-based (home-based) uses of your time:
Read. Trade journals, self-help books, positive attitude books, sales books, *The Business Journal*, annual reports and brochures of your biggest customers, anything humorous, trend-setting books. *Study*.
Listen. Self-help tapes. Nightingale Conant (Chicago) has a catalog of thousands of hours of profound, impactful information. *Invest*.
Mastermind. Attract smart friends and associates to your house once a week to create new ideas and action plans. *Invite*.
Compute. This includes writing, planning, and learning, and inter-netting. The computer is the biggest link to the 21st century -- master it. *Explore*.

The next time you say "I don't have enough time," substitute that phrase with "I don't choose to spend my time in that manner." It's closer to the truth. The *real* truth is, you're not investing your time in the most important person in the world -- you!

GetReal...

If you devoted the time to *learning* that you
currently spend *watching*, you could be an international
expert on *anything*. Me? I studied sales and wrote
about sales instead of watching the news.

After 2.5 years, I published my first book,
The Sales Bible.
Which do you think helped my career more --
reading and writing for an hour each morning
for 2.5 years, or watching the news?

And what are you doing with your hour?

JustTryThis...

Pick something you love
and do it an hour a day
for a year.

The idea for this story came from my friend, Theo Androus.

DON'T WORRY, COLLEGE WILL PREPARE YOU FOR THE REAL WORLD.

They lied. When you were in high school they said, "Take these courses and you'll be ready for college." They lied. When you were in college they said, "Take these courses and you'll be ready for the real world." They lied.

How many courses did you take in positive attitude, goal setting, responsibility, listening, pride, and understanding others? How important are those lessons in the successful execution of your job function?

The courses you really need, they never gave. Why? Bad question. Heaven forbid we should make academia accountable for an individual's preparation for the real world, or responsible for offering the educational programs we really need for career and life success. NOTE: I'm not saying abandon what we've got, I'm recommending we *supplement* the stuff that makes us excellent Trivial Pursuit and Jeopardy players (Geography, Literature, History), for the information and lessons we could really use (Attitude, Goals, Responsibility).

If you're in customer service, or sales, or management there's a set of *fundamental beginner* skills to master in order to succeed at any job. These fundamental educational elements are prerequisites to the actual serving or selling process. They give you the background and understanding to succeed at any task. Asking you to manage, sell, or serve without these skills is like asking you to do algebra without knowing how to add and subtract. Impossible.

Here's a list of subjects that will prepare you for success in relationships, the working world, and life. Imagine the fun you could have had in school if it was real-world oriented. How many of these courses have you had?

1. The Magic of Creating a Positive Attitude. We become what we think about. The magic of creating a positive attitude. The secret of success. Building quality performance that starts with a positive attitude. *Why not offer a course on how to establish and maintain one?*

2. Setting and Exceeding Goals. Everyone knows they should set goals -- very few know how. Don't confuse activity with accomplishment. Goals are the road map to success. Selecting and exceeding goals increases chances for success and personal satisfaction. *When's the last time you took a goal-setting course?*

3. Establishing Pride on the Job. Having pride in yourself, your company, and what you do. Liking yourself, your job, and your career. Building a belief system. *Developing pride skills is critical, especially in service.*

4. Understanding People. Sometimes people need our help but have a strange way of expressing it. A brisk walk in the other person's shoes to better understand how to deal with them. *This course is the gateway to customer service and sales.*

5. Taking Responsibility. For your actions, what happens to you, and the success of your company. If you think everyone else is at fault except you...think again. How to accept and take responsibility. *Take ownership of your job and your dealings with customers and co-workers.*

6. Effective Listening. The best way to know how to serve a customer or help a co-worker is to listen. The vital importance of listening with the intent to understand, and then with the intent to respond. *Listening is the weakest personal development skill we possess.*

7. Effective Communication. Communicating to be understood. Co-workers and customers want clear, concise information. Communication skills are the most important, and least taught skills in the universe. *Why?*

8. Embracing Change. Change occurs every day -- and it's resisted -- often fought, even though it's often better than what we now have. *We need to teach the ability of how to capture the opportunity of change.*

9. Building Friendships and Long-Term Relationships. Establishing, building and maintaining relationships that last. Methods and techniques to build respect, friendships, and relationships with co-workers and customers. *The "value first" method of dealing with others.*

10. Making Effective Decisions. Gaining the ability to make effective decisions (which means taking risks). Why and how decisions are made. The steps of effective decision making is combined with the

Lessons You Never Learned in School 16

message that it's OK to make mistakes. *Taking responsibility without fear and guilt.*

11. Working as a Team. You can't make it alone. The power of one plus one is ten times greater than two. *Understanding how teams work individually and collectively will lead to success.*

That's the curriculum I recommend. Wish I ran the schools. Oops, better run my own life first. If you're ready to resign your position as *general manager of the universe,* and want to get these lessons instead of blaming others -- you'll have to seek out self-help or professionally developed programs.

Thank goodness you are responsible for your own success. Take control of your own personal development to achieve your goals and dreams -- while the school systems continue to wallow in their own mediocrity, and persist in telling the big lie. Jim Rohn has a challenge quote -- "With formal education you can earn a living, with self education, you can earn a fortune!"

GetReal...
Which one are you earning?

THE WINDS. THE TIDES. THE JOB. THE CAREER. THEY ALL CHANGE.

A career in service means adapt to change or die. Changes occur in the business world (and your job) every minute.

Why do so few people rise to the top? Because they are unable to synergize superior personal skills with the flexibility to adapt to the ever-changing facets of their job in conjunction with company and family. (Read that again.) A person's ability to accept and roll with the tides of change, are at the fulcrum of his or her ability to succeed.

Here are the defined areas of "business" change. I have added SUCCESS TACTICS for each area to help you utilize these elements of change to your best advantage.

Product/Service Changes. This is the easiest change to accept. Usually it means newer and better. *SUCCESS TACTICS: Immediately learn and master the changes. Determine what new competitive advantages these changes bring. Look for ways your customer will benefit from these changes and focus on them.*

Policy Changes. New rules. New procedures. *SUCCESS TACTICS: Don't swim upstream. Fighting policy changes leads to employment changes. Spend as much time figuring out a way to use the new procedures to your advantage as you do griping about them.*

Price Changes. The price goes up. *SUCCESS TACTICS: Stop talking price. Talk value. Talk cost over a period of time. (When they raise the price of a Mercedes $2,000 do they lose market share? No. -- Neither should you.)*

Market Condition Changes. There's not enough demand for your product. Now what? *SUCCESS TACTICS: Fight harder to increase your customer base. Network more. Sell like it was your survival. (It is.) Start an hour earlier. Stay an hour later. Utilize your time to its maximum. Don't blame the conditions for your inability to get the job done.*

Competition Changes. Your competitor lowers prices and talks trash about you. You find this out from your best customer -- who your competitor has just stolen. *SUCCESS TACTICS: Find out why. Make the changes necessary to ensure that it never happens again. Then find out where your competitive advantages lie and sell from them.*

Lessons You Never Learned in School

16

Customer Changes. New buyer. New owner. Change in business stability. New growth. *SUCCESS TACTICS: Determine how this change affects you. If there is a new person, become a resource to help him or her understand their new corporate culture from your perspective.*

Company Changes. Sometimes it's difficult to produce when the structure of the company, or the internal organization changes. Partner buyouts. Internal restructuring (re-engineering). Changing the corporate culture you've become secure with. *SUCCESS TACTICS: Now is the time to seek to understand and harmonize. Don't fight it. Be proactive toward acceptance. Ask how you can help. Support the leader. Don't grumble to anyone.*

Pay Changes. If you don't care about being the best -- pay is everything. Look beyond the paycheck and ask yourself, "Will this job lead to my long-term success?" *SUCCESS TACTICS: Figure out what it really means to you from a workload and a dollars-and-cents position. Is the change acceptable to you? Can you live with it? It may be time to look to another company -- or start your own.*

Staff Changes. People come and go. If your friend is fired or a real jerk gets hired, it can cause a lot of stress. *SUCCESS TACTICS: Look at why the change took place. Look at the last few changes. Is there a trend? Are you next? What do you need to do to get to the top?*

Personal Growth Changes. Marriage. Divorce. Kids. Death. Too much debt. Desire to excel. *SUCCESS TACTICS: Leave your personal problems at home. Maintain your success focus -- goal achievement may take a renewed effort. Listen to positive attitude tapes every second you're in the car.*

Often you cannot affect the change... It affects you. Your responsibility in dealing with the changing elements of life and career is to:
• understand them first (no knee jerk reactions).
• create the attitude of acceptance.
• view change as a challenge and learning experience.
• make a plan to harmonize with those things or people that affect you.
• speak about changes in a supportive way.
• focus on adaptability -- your ability to compromise.
• act on changes in a building way.
• maintain your positive attitude at all costs.
• don't allow change to divert your focus and drive to succeed.
• adopt the attitude that you will take advantage of change.

New is better... We buy "new" in the grocery store. It's the second most powerful marketing word (*free* is first). If people crave it in the store, eat it up on TV, why do they resist it -- actually fight it on the job? Here's why:
• Fear of the unknown.
• Fear of loss of existing security.
• Poor attitude toward growth.
• Lack of self-confidence that they can adapt.
• Lack of desire or personal motivation to change.

Don't get trapped... There are pitfalls to beware of. Others may not be able to take change like you can. Don't get caught up in their ~~crap~~ trap.
• Don't join their pity party.
• Don't agree with their plight.
• Suggest good things or solutions.
• Offer a meeting to discuss and uncover opportunities.

Add one *new inevitable* -- to the original two -- (death and taxes).
Change. Harness its power and succeed -- fight it and fail.

...
Your ability to accept change
is at the fulcrum of your ability
to succeed.

Lessons You Never Learned in School 16

10.5 WAYS TO ADAPT TO

change

and incorporate it naturally into your life -- and your life's work.

1. **Just accept change as part of life** -- It's inevitable -- don't fight it. Give change a chance.
2. **Keep change in perspective** -- It ain't brain cancer -- it's not death. It's something new and different. It might be better.
3. **Look for new opportunities to succeed** -- You'll never see how change can work in your favor if you're mad.
4. **Write down all the bad things that could possibly happen** -- And figure out a game plan to avert or deal with each one of them.
5. **Write down all the good things that can come of change** -- And expand on the opportunities they can bring you and your company.
6. **Discuss your concerns with others WHO CAN HELP** -- Avoid those who are grumbling or wallowing in self-pity.
7. **Don't "WOE IS ME" it** -- Seek out others less fortunate than you to keep things in perspective.
8. **Form a team to figure out positive outcomes** -- Explore as much possible good from change as you (and others) are able.
9. **Keep your attitude level and reinforcement at an all time high** -- Now is the time to listen and read as much positive mental attitude things as you can. Keep your car cassette player full of positive words from the masters.
10. **Goal three things that will make the change work** -- Then go on an all out action plan to achieve those goals.
10.5 **Remember that you're the greatest** --This change is an opportunity to prove it to yourself, and achieve new greatness. Just roll along -- just change it.

I wanna be a success! I wanna be a success!

There is no quick fix, magic wand, or potion that will give you the success you're dreaming for.

So, what's the secret of success? Well -- it's not a single secret -- it's a secret formula. Here is a series of 18.5 principles, strategies, and actions that will lead you to success.

OK, OK, the *Secrets of Success* are not real secrets, they're fundamental steps that successful people have been executing for centuries. These are attributes that high achievers have in common. *Here are the 18.5 Secrets of Success; and more important, a challenge for you to rate yourself in each element -- (1=lowest, 10=highest). How well have you mastered each of these characteristics so far?*

1. **Believe you can.** High achievers have the mental posture for success -- believing they are capable of achieving it. This belief must extend to their product and their company. A strong belief system seems obvious -- but few people possess it. Too many people look outside (for the money they can make) rather than look inside (for the money they can earn). To believe that you're the best and that you're capable of high achievement is the hardest thing to do. It requires daily dedication to self-support, self-encouragement, and positive self-talk.

2. **Create the environment.** The right home and work environment will encourage you. Supportive spouse, family members, and co-workers will make the road to success a smooth ride. It's up to you to create it.

3. **Have the right associations.** Hang around the right people. Other successful people. Network where your best customers and prospects go. Join the right associations. Make the right friends. Stay away from poison people -- the ones who can't seem to get anywhere. Have a mentor or three. Who do you hang around with? That is who you are likely to become.

4. **Expose yourself to what's new.** If you're not learning every day -- your competition is. New information is essential to success (unless you're like most people, who already know everything -- lucky you).

5. **Plan for the day.** Since you don't know on which day success will occur, you'd better be ready every day. Prepare with education. Plan with goals, and the details for their achievement. "Learn" and "goal" are the surest methods to be ready for your success.

6. **Become valuable.** The more valuable you become, the more the marketplace will reward you. Give first. Become known as a resource. Your value is linked to your knowledge and your willingness to help others.

7. **Have the answers your customers need.** The more you can solve problems, the easier path you will have to success. People don't want excuses, they want answers. In order to have those answers, you must have superior knowledge about what you do -- and explain it in terms of the customer's needs.

8. **Recognize opportunity.** Stay alert for the situations that can create success opportunities. A positive attitude allows you to see the possibilities when opportunity strikes -- because it often shows up in the form of adversity.

9. **Take advantage of opportunity.** Recognizing opportunity is hard. Acting on it is harder. Opportunity is elusive. It exists all over the place, but very few can see it. Some people fear it because it involves change, most don't believe they are capable of achievement.

10. **Take responsibility.** We all blame others to a degree. Blame is tied to success in reverse proportion. The lower your degree of blame -- the higher degree of success you'll achieve. Get the job done yourself no matter what. Petty blame is rampant and the biggest waste of time. Don't blame others or yourself. Take responsibility for your actions and decisions. Blaming others is an easy thing to do, but leads to mediocrity. Successful people take responsibility for everything they do AND everything that happens to them.

11. **Take action.** *Just do it* (Nike) is the expression for the 90's. Actions are the only way to bridge plans and goals with accomplishment. Nothing happens until you do something to make it happen -- every day.

☐ **12. Make mistakes.** The best teacher is failure. It's the rudest of awakenings, and the breeding ground for self-determination. Don't think of them as mistakes -- think of them as *learning experiences not to be repeated.*

☐ **13. Willing to risk.** This is the most crucial factor. *No risk, no reward* is the biggest understatement in the business world. It should be stated -- *no risk, no nothing.* Taking chances is a common thread among every successful person. Most people won't risk because (they think) they *fear the unknown.* The real reason people won't risk is that they lack the preparation and education that breeds the self-confidence (self-belief) to take a chance. Risk is the basis of success. If you want to succeed, you'd better be willing to risk whatever it takes to get there.

☐ **14. Keep your eye on the prize.** Post your goals. Stay focused on your dreams and they will become reality. Too many foolish diversions will take you farther from your goals.

☐ **15. Balance yourself.** Your physical, spiritual, and emotional health are vital to your success quest. Plan your time to allow your personal goals to be synergized with your work goals.

☐ **16. Invest, don't spend.** You should spend 10-20% LESS than you earn. Clip your credit cards in half and make a few investments -- with professional guidance.

☐ **17. Stick at it till you win.** Most people fail because they quit too soon. Don't let that be you. Make a plan AND a commitment to see the plan through -- no matter what. Don't quit on the ten-yard line. Have whatever it takes to score.

☐ **18. Develop and maintain a positive attitude.** Surprisingly this is not a common characteristic. By the time many make it to the top, they have developed irreversible cynicism. But positive attitude makes achieving success much easier -- and more fun.

☐ **18.5 Ignore idiots and zealots.** Also known as pukers, these people will try to rain on your parade (discourage you) because they have no parade of their own. Avoid them at all costs.

Lessons You Never Learned in School   16

See, I told you -- no revelations. OK, so if these characteristics seem so simple, how come they're so difficult to master? Answer: your lack of personal self-discipline and a dedication to life-long learning. Oh yeah, that.

I am consistently amazed and disappointed at the small number of people willing to execute the simple, daily self-disciplines needed to reach higher levels of success. They know it will bring them the success they dream about, yet they fail to execute.

In any business effort, or career position, the person who will emerge victorious most of the time is the person who wants it the most. Victory does not always go to the swift (hare vs. tortoise), victory does not always go to the powerful (David vs. Goliath), and victory does not always go to the lowest price (Yugo vs. Mercedes).

The victory we call success goes to the best prepared, self-believing, self-confident, right-associated, self-taught, responsible person who sees the opportunity and is willing to take a risk to seize it -- sometimes a big risk. Is that you?

Well, there's the secret -- and it's not real complicated. It's not nuclear physics or brain surgery. And now that I've shared it with thousands of people, you'd think there would be a surge in the ratio of successful people. Nope.

(Get Real)...

The reason the success formula is considered a secret is that it remains an *enigma*. It seems that there's very few people who are willing to put forth the *effort* to get from where they are to where they want to be. Most make excuses and blame others for their own poor choices.

The biggest secret (and the biggest obstacle) to success is *you*.
The formula is there for everyone to know -- BUT, there's a big difference between knowing what to do, and doing it.

"The biggest reason people don't succeed is because they don't expose themselves to existing information."
JEFF OLSON, CEO THE PEOPLES NETWORK

12.5 PRINCIPLES OF LIFE-LONG LEARNING

Rate yourself in the box to the left of each principle
(1=poor, 2=average, 3=good, 4=very good, 5=the greatest)
(1=never, 2=rarely, 3=sometimes, 4=frequently, 5=always)

☐ 1. It starts with a positive attitude... Learn how to achieve one. Gather information on positive people in your library.

Napoleon Hill	Dale Carnegie	W. Clement Stone
Maxwell Maltz	Wayne Dyer	Earl Nightingale
Norman Vincent Peale	Jim Rohn	

☐ 2. Listen to audio tapes -- own several sets and play them in your car.

☐ 3. Read books -- build your library one (read) book a month.

☐ 4. Attend live seminars -- as many as you can afford, as often as you can.

☐ 5. Join Toastmasters -- 90 minutes of speaking & self-evaluation a week.

☐ 6. Record yourself speaking -- a weekly ritual.

☐ 7. Record yourself reading -- a weekly ritual.

☐ 8. Record yourself on the phone or with a customer -- a weekly ritual.

☐ 9. Record your personal commercial -- a weekly ritual.

☐ 10. Record your own set of customer service tapes (by reading this book into a cassette recorder). Get great at serving and presenting at the same time.

☐ 11. Listen to your own tapes as much as you listen to others.

☐ 12. Spend 30 minutes a day learning something new.

☐ 12.5 Practice what you've learned as soon as you learn it.

Score: 65-70=WOW!   60-64=AOK
40-59=Get Help!   20-39=Start Over

Lessons You Never Learned in School **16**

THREE PRINCIPLES THAT LEAD TO SUCCESS AND WEALTH.

Many people get into a career to "make money." There could not be a worse reason to enter a profession. The best way amass a lot of money in a career is to earn it.

NOTE WELL: I did not say *make money*. In serving others you don't make money -- you earn it. The biggest reason people fail is the philosophy, "I'm in this to make money," or "I'm in this because that's where the money is."

Everyone wants to earn a million dollars. Each of us for different reasons -- but we all need money to achieve our goals and dreams. How do you get the money? By living and executing the three principles of wealth building:
1. You earn money by building a strong self-belief system.
2. You earn money by being better than the rest.
3. You earn money by having answers that others don't.

Here's a brief overview of each principle.
Building belief is... Having the confidence that you can do whatever you set your mind to do. Knowing *why* you want to earn a fortune, and living the dream by having the confidence to take action. How are you building that belief now?
Being better than the rest is... Doing whatever it takes to excel at what you do. Getting up one hour earlier. Striving to be the best at everything, and not be willing to settle for second place. There is no prize for second place in job promotions.
Learning new answers is... Exposing yourself to success information that you don't now have -- but need to be the best. Seminars, books, tapes -- a plan of life-long learning. There is only one way to get answers: *by learning them.* It seems simple -- just not easy. Some people have to go through failure to get them. Some have a steady diet of exposing themselves to new information every day. The key is *learning something new every day.*

How are you getting those answers now? Have you put yourself in a position to get the knowledge you need -- to earn the money you want to achieve your dreams?

"The biggest reason people don't succeed is that they don't expose themselves to existing information," says Jeff Olson, CEO of The Peoples Network. And I add to that -- *"Therefore, they don't believe in themselves enough (lack the confidence) to succeed."*

It's not so important that you *want* to succeed -- it's critical that you know *why* you want to succeed. What has *prevented* you from achieving your success to date? What *belief system and game plan* do you need to put in place to gain that success?

WARNING: If you read the last paragraph and blamed everyone and everything but yourself, you are doomed. Take responsibility for the failure -- and do something about it (I'll guarantee that when you succeed you'll take the responsibility).

It's easy to lose self-belief, if the one you've got in place is weak due to poor knowledge and lack of determination. It's easy to fail at your job if you have never told yourself (sold yourself) the real reason you want success in the first place. Not earning money for money's sake -- but *the real reason you want the money, and what you'll do with it once you get it.*

For example, you may want money for a specific college that you want your child to attend, it may be to liberate you from a spouse, it may be to say "HA!" to a sibling or a parent. Whatever it is -- uncover it, write it down, post it up (if possible), carry it with you, read it twice a day -- and then you will begin to live it.

Combine your "why" with the desire and dedication to be the best, and presto -- career success.

Get Real ...

Some of you are reading this and saying,
"Jeffrey, don't bug me with this philosophy stuff,
tell me how to make more money."
I am.
This is the most powerful lesson I can deliver.
Only a few will get it --
the ones who will rise to the top.

Loyal.

The

most

valuable

of

your

customer's

virtues.

LOYALTY LESSONS FROM THE REAL WORLD

(LESSONS YOU CAN CONVERT INTO YOUR SUCCESS)

- Converting satisfied customers to loyal customers
- The chef would like you to try some of this
- Creating and documenting your own success stories

CONVERTING SATISFIED CUSTOMERS TO LOYAL CUSTOMERS -- SPINNING STRAW INTO GOLD.

Your ability to convert your satisfied customers into loyal customers is the fulcrum of your long-term success, both as a company and as an employee.

The company wants loyal customers to ensure a solid customer base and long-term growth. The employee wants loyal customers to ensure employment (no customers, no reason to come to work).

The conversion begins to come about when the company and its people DECIDE to start doing it -- not before. Until they decide -- customers will be "satisfied." Converting "satisfied" customers to "loyal" is an action-driven process, not something that just "happens." Someone (lots of someones) must MAKE it happen.

Growing Loyal Customers...
I wish there were a package of seeds you could buy that would just grow if you planted them on the right day and watered and weeded them. Well, as far-fetched as this sounds -- that's close to the formula. It's not planting -- more like nurturing. Your nurturing determines how strong they are devoted to you. "Deep Rooted" if you will.

There's no "instant" way to grow loyal customers.
There is a slow-but-sure way...
You don't grow loyalty in a day;
You grow loyalty day-by-day.

Creating a Corps of Ambassadors...
Customers who act on your behalf to build your business. Customers acting like salespeople, customer service people, PR people, advertising people, stockholders, and owners of your business.

There is no "instant" way to create Ambassadors.
There is a slow-but-sure way...
You don't earn loyalty in a day;
You earn loyalty day-by-day.

Double your business with loyal customers referring new customers...
You could double your business if you just got every one of your present customers to refer ONE more customer just like themselves. Imagine your phone ringing with people wanting to buy. Imagine people walking into your business wanting to buy.

> There is no "instant" way to create referrals.
> There is a slow-but-sure way...
> You don't earn referrals in a day;
> You earn referrals day-by-day.

The secret for earning loyal customers...
HINT: It has to do with how Rome was built.

> There is no "instant" way to earn loyalty.
> There is a slow-but-sure way...
> You don't earn loyalty in a day;
> You earn loyalty day-by-day.

The next 25 pages are loaded
with answers that will help you
convert your customers from
"satisfied" to "loyal."
One hitch...
you must add yourself.
Answers require implementation.
The only way loyalty "happens"
is if YOU make it happen.

THE REAL CHALLENGE OF LOYALTY...

Make me *want* to come back.
Make me *want* to tell others.

The chef would like you to try some of this...

Julio and I walked into *Emeril's* Restaurant in New Orleans. It was a pretty classy place. We sat down and our waiter approached our table. I expected the traditional "Hi, my name is Jason and I'll be your server tonight. Can I get you something from the bar?" Crap. "Start you off with an appetizer?" Crap. "Tell you about our specials?" Crap.

To my surprise, he was carrying two small (well-decorated) plates of food. "The chef would like you to try some of this," the waiter said with pride, and placed the plates in front of us. WOW!

I eat out 1,000 meals a year. In the last ten thousand meals, the chef never asked me to try squat. I was speechless, floored, and excited all at once.

The meal, as you could imagine was superb, the service was superb. During the meal, the chefs in the kitchen came out into the restaurant to take a bow -- the place went wild with applause. I gave them a standing ovation.

Now the main course is over, Julio and I are stuffed -- but craving something sweet. (Ever have that feeling?) So, I say to our waiter, "I'm full up to the Adam's apple, but do you have just a small something-sweet in the kitchen?"

"Say no more!" says the waiter with a flair. In three minutes he returns with a plate full of a miniature portion of every dessert on the menu. And two spoons, and two forks. Cool. Way cool. Unbelievably cool.

We tipped the waiter $50.00 (40%) and I felt like we stiffed him.

Get Real...

Do you have any idea how many people I tell about "the chef would like you to try some of this?" Everyone I can get to listen. And they all ask the same question -- "What was the name of that restaurant again?" I spell it real slow -- E-M-E-R-I-L-S.

CAPTURE YOUR SUCCESS STORIES IN EVERY WAY POSSIBLE.

Document success.
Replicate loyal actions.
Tell everyone.

When you do something memorable in your company or your life, very few people ever know about it (far fewer than when you screw up).

Why?

Simple answer -- you didn't tell anyone. You just expect people to find out on their own. Big mistake.

When you do something great, or something great happens, capture it and reproduce it for all to see.

When a memorable event occurs within your company or with a customer, here are the avenues of exposure you can capture for others (including all your customers) to see your accomplishments.
• A letter of testimony.
• An audio taped interview.
• An article in the newspaper.
• An article in your newsletter.
• An article in the customer's newsletter.
• A call-in talk-show report.
• A blurb on the news.
• As part of a testimonial advertising campaign.
• A video shot in the customer's location using your product.

Once you capture the event, maximize it.

Duplicate the Duplication.
You get an article published in the *Business Journal* about your great service. WOW! You read it, your staff reads it, and you hope all your customers, prospects, and competitors read it -- but they don't.

What do you do? Easy. Duplicate the article (professionally) and send it to EVERYONE. Put it in EVERY piece of outgoing mail for the next two months. Do a customer/prospect mailing. Do a target mailing. Do a broadcast fax. Repeat the best quote from the story in other ads. In short, maximize your good fortune and build good image at the same time.

Perhaps I've put the cart before the horse. The only way you can get these memorable events to take place is to create them. That may be too much of an assumption on my part. You may not be creating opportunities for stories of success.

Look around. What's going on at your place? Anything? Anything exceptional? Anything newsworthy or worth bragging about to others who may be attracted to your business? Well, that's the acid test. First there must be the prospect of something worthy of bragging about.

Now I'm not talking about a new product announcement. That means nothing to anyone except you. The things I'm referring to are memorable stories, exceptional service, unusual situations, and items of value to your customers and prospects.

Hint on creating stories:
• Do something of value.
• Do something helpful.
• Do something giving.
• Do something unexpected.
• Do something creative.

Create your own stories of success doing something proactive (before prompted to do so). Then document the stories, replicate (duplicate) them, and tell everyone you know.

Customers and prospects will love your success -- especially if you combine it with theirs. There is only one group of people that will hate your success -- your competition.
Don't you love it?

Loyalty --
The Final
Frontier

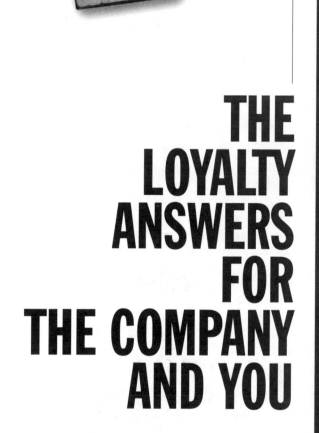

THE
LOYALTY
ANSWERS
FOR
THE COMPANY
AND YOU

- Loyalty is the breed and you are the stud
- Make one customer ecstatic --
  one mind-boggle a day
- Take a few short leaps and you're at loyalty
- The Loyalty Solution
- The Measurement for Loyalty
- A measuring device:
  Be your own customer

LOYAL CUSTOMERS ARE A BREED -- AND YOU ARE THE STUD.

If customer satisfaction is at an all-time high, why is customer loyalty at an all-time low?

Simple -- satisfied customers will shop anywhere -- satisfaction is not any indication that the customer will repeat a purchase. As a consumer, you have often been satisfied, yet never returned to that place of business.

A more complicated reason is that business is just now discovering that *satisfaction* is no longer the measure of customer success -- loyalty is.

What is a loyal customer? One who will create positive word-of-mouth advertising about you, refer other people to do business with you, and fight before they switch from you to a competitor.

Well, Jeffrey, how do you make customers loyal to you? Is it low price? No, the second someone offers a lower price, the customer becomes "loyal" to that lowest price. There's more to loyalty than money. Money is usually the bait used to lure "satisfied" customers from their present supplier. The lower the satisfaction, the more they'll take the bait.

Loyal occurs when you're first on the mind of the customer when they want what you sell -- a satisfied customer is the last to tell you they decided to buy someplace else. Loyal, first to know -- satisfied, last to know. Hmmmm.

Loyal is best understood when related to the word "fan." When you go to a college, or grow up in a city, you are a loyal "fan" of their sporting teams. Fan is short for fanatic. How many fanatic customers do you have?

Sports loyalty is when you love one team -- and HATE their arch rival (their main competition). Who loves you?

To make it even more complex, loyalty is not the result of a single experience or event. If it were, everyone would go out and do it. Loyalty evolves -- like loyalty to a spouse or friend. It matures (or dissolves) over time, based on your deeds, actions, and words.

So how do you get customers to be loyal to you or your business? Since loyalty doesn't just "happen," the answer is a question: What are the elements that breed loyalty? Here are a few:

- **Being unusual where usual is expected.** Changing the boring stuff you do every day to WOW! the customer and create atmosphere where the customer "has to" tell others how great it was. Fax cover sheet, voice mail, phone greeting, invoices. Standard stuff you change to SET the new standard.
- **Getting business for your customers and prospects.** If you want to build loyalty beyond belief -- just start GETTING your customers hot leads and prospects that turn into business for them. Then, when you call your customers, they won't know if you're buying or selling.
- **Giving your customers and prospects valuable information to help build their business.** Your customers want answers, not always more of your product. If you want customers forever, become valuable, become a resource they can't live without.
- **Give proactive service.** Calling customers to tell them they need service or supplies just before they were about to call you. Letting them know when the "deals" are coming up. Doing something so memorable for them, so that they call others and tell them about you.
- **Service way beyond the sale.** Offering product-use tips and information that help your customer build her business or achieve her goals.
- **Give the best service they've ever had.** Having great service is at the heart of the loyalty process. Service that starts with yes, provides solutions and ends with WOW!
- **Give friendly service.** How important is friendly? Ask yourself where you LOVE to do business, and I'll bet everyone there is friendly. Your customers want the same from you.
- **Answering the phone and helping in a memorable way.** How do you feel an automated computer phone answering system sets with customers? How do you like it? Does it breed or erode loyalty? Saving money by not having someone human greet your customers is the twentieth century's single best example of "penny wise, dollar foolish." Customers call for one reason -- they want help. Why give them the hell of the computer?

The Loyalty Answers for The Company and You 18

- **Give something they'll use every day and show to others.** Delivering an ad specialty that's so distinctive that they'll show or tell others. The difference between a coffee mug that sits in a drawer and one that's shown to everyone is about $2.00. If it's shown to twenty other people, that's just 10¢ per WOW!
- **Going beyond the expected.** They expect a delivery fee? Set it up for free. They expect two-week delivery? Get it for them the next day.
- **Being fun, unusual, creative, and poignant.** Being human in the world of business can set you apart more than you know. Become likable, and people will like to do business with you.

RECRUIT LOYAL CUSTOMERS ONE AT A TIME -- ONE DAY AT A TIME.

Suppose you decided to make one customer ecstatic every day. What would happen?

Well, the first few days -- nothing.

Then, after a week or two, people would start to call and re-order. You'd start to get thank-you letters, unsolicited referrals, and things that prove the customer you made ecstatic was breeding their loyalty. People in your company would be having fun (heaven forbid) making customers feel great.

Let's define "ecstatic." Here's examples of "how-to" --
• Select at random "The Customer of the Day." An award that's a complete surprise and gives you and the customer a reason to celebrate.
• Award a plaque or certificate and a nice gift. Something they'll keep on their desk (like a CLASSY coffee mug with your name on it AND theirs.

You offer special pricing, freebies, discounts, lunches -- whatever it takes to get him or her talking. And they will talk.

Now let's say that every person in your company was on the same program -- make one customer ecstatic every day. The concept doesn't seem that complex or expensive. Wouldn't take that long either -- just spend a few extra moments and do a few extra things for ONE customer a day.

But the concept, when applied to the numbers, is staggering. If there are twenty people in your company, that would be 100 customers a week. Five thousand two hundred customers a year. WOW!

The easiest way to breed a loyal army is to recruit them one at a time -- here's the magic answer -- have every person in your company who talks to customers "make one customer ecstatic every day."

This is one of the most real and simplest answers in this book. And the best part is that you can begin to do it right now -- on your own.

You don't need permission from a boss
to make a customer feel great.

Just Try This...

Take a few short leaps and you're at Loyalty

Leap Number 1
Start out as the happiest, friendliest, most important person in the world.

Leap Number 2
Set the right tone from the first three words.
Start with positive words.

Leap Number 3
Serve them so they remember it and tell others.

Leap Number 4
Keep up your communication with them after the transaction.

Leap Number 5
Continue to offer value without expectation of return, and you win.

Leap Number 5.5
Do it for the most important person in the world.
You. Be your best.

What will it take to end measuring **"satisfaction"** in your business?

All of your

competitors'

customers

becoming

loyal

to your

competition.

THE LOYALTY SOLUTION IS REAL SIMPLE.
Not real easy.

1. **Change your survey to "loyalty-based" questions and responses.** In most cases all you need to do is add the words "why" or "how" to the front of your existing "customer satisfaction survey."

2. **Have the staff necessary to document and interpret the information.** Your customers will be answering in sentence form. This means someone will have to read the answers, transpose them to a computer, and distribute them to the people they affect.

3. **Meet regularly to determine what needs to change.** Vote on what and in what order new actions will be taken. If you just implement one suggestion or new strategy a week, at the end of the year you're 52 ways better than you were.

4. **Have the money and the staff necessary to turn the information into action.** Talking about things is way different from doing them. Most of the time new ideas are not implemented because of a "lack of budget," or it's evil twin, "lack of manpower."

5. **Adjust your advertising budgets and customer retention budgets to at least equal.** This may be the hardest task. Take half your advertising budgets and spend it on existing customers. Create an army of people talking about you -- not a bunch of self-righteous drivel about "we're the greatest."

6. **Benchmark (document) all your daily customer interactions and develop a "best response" for each one.** Each person handles the same situation with different words and actions. Wrong. Document the best way to handle the top 25 customer interfaces in your business and train your people to do it the best way EVERY time.

6.5 **Your employees care about themselves, not you.** Train your people to be the best they can be for themselves, before you brainwash them with a bunch of your policy crap. If you help them be the best they can be for themselves, then (and only then) can you teach them the "best responses" for each situation they're likely to incur.

How do you
measure loyalty?
Only ONE way.

The measurement of
loyalty success
is...

unsolicited referrals
and re-orders.

*How do you get
unsolicited
referrals?*

YOU
EARN
THEM!

A **"GET REAL"–"JUST TRY THIS"** Measuring Device

Want a real report card? Be careful, it may hurt. It may hurt bad. It may hurt real bad. Still want it? OK...

Be your own customer
once a month.

I learned this by accident from a hotel general manager. Remember my "nightmare" stay at the Sheraton Westport in St. Louis?

I had a real rude front-desk person, no luggage cart, no ironing board, no internet data-port -- and the handwritten "exceed your expectations" note from the general manager on my pillow. And I said, "Next time, please do not exceed my expectations, just meet them."

I asked the GM, "By the way, when's the last time you stayed here at the Sheraton Westport Hotel?" And, he said, "Oh, I've never stayed here."

Think he would have ever written that "exceed your expectations" note if he did? I said, "Listen, why don't you check in at 9:30 tomorrow night with a bunch of bags, some wrinkled clothing, try to get on the Internet, and see what happens to you. Do that before you write your next note to a guest."

None of the stuff would have happened if the general manager would have been a guest in his own hotel -- if he had "been his own customer."

So the thought struck me that "be your own customer" would be a great measuring device for any business. Yours, for example.

How easy is it to do business with you? Are your customers all on the same schedule as you? How easy is it to get help at your company? Get an answer? Resolve a problem? The answer is -- you probably don't know, because you've never tried.

GetReal...

How can you know how to sell and serve if you don't know
what the customer's experience has been? Answer: *You can't.*

JustTryThis...

Here's how "be your own customer" works. First, pretend
you're a big customer. One your company would be hurt by if lost.
Then pick up the phone from outside the office and select
from one of the 18.5 options below...

1   Call 30 minutes before work officially begins. *(Get a dumb or rude recording?)*
2. Call after hours -- in most cases just wait until 5 minutes after people go home *(Able to reach a human?)*
3. Try to place an after (or before) hours order. *(Able to do it -- or do you have to have someone call you back at THEIR convenience?)*
4. Try to place an after (or before) hours service call. *(Get help or get frustrated?)*
5. Call during lunch. *(Put through to their voice mail without a request to do so?)*
6. Ask for the president during working hours. See if you can get through. *(How easy is it? How accessible is the president's office to a customer? Get a "what's this in reference to?")*
7. Try to place an order during working hours. *(How easy is it? How pleasant is it?)*
    variation: Order something you're out of.
    variation: Order something you don't carry.
    variation: Ask who else sells the stuff you do.
    variation: Try to get a lower price.
    variation: Try to get a reference from others you do business with.
    variation: Try to get someone to "sell" you because you're hesitant.
8. Press the "automated" numbers. *(How easy is it to find your way? How long did it take?)*
9. Test your ease of voice mail. *(If you get lost in the voice-mail loop -- press "0" and see what happens. Try pressing "0" after hours and see what happens.)*
10. Call with a gripe -- have a complaint during the day. *(Was it handled in a memorable way?)*
11. Call up angry -- get rude. *(Did it end up good or bad?)*

12. Have a billing problem. *(Did it end up good or bad?)*
13. Have a delivery problem. *(Did it end up good or bad?)*
14. Have a quality problem. *(Did it end up good or bad?)*
15. When you call during the day, how friendly is the receptionist?
16. When you call during the day, how helpful is the receptionist?
17. Try to get someone to take a message for you. *(The latest corporate joke. People will not take a message -- they will insist you leave a voice mail.)*
18. Ask for someone, get your call transferred and see if you automatically (rudely) get transferred to a voice mail.
18.5 Call and ask for yourself when you're out of the office.

HARD QUESTIONS: *Was anything so memorable that you had to tell someone else how great it was? Did ANYTHING memorable happen? If no, start over.*

GetReal...
If you don't know what the customer experiences, how can you understand them when they need help -- have a problem -- or want to order?

JustTryThis...
Count how many times you get passed around, referred to a voice mail, told what can't be done, or get an unfriendly or unhelpful person.

GetReal,Real...
How does it feel to be a customer? Did you like the way you were treated? What does it take to get to a live human being at your company? How do you think your customer would like it? How do you think they would rate the experience? How did you rate it?

JustTryThis...
Select the 5 worst problems your customers face, and live them.

JustTryThis...
Spend a day at your customer's using your own product.

Get Real, Real, Real ...
The best, most funniest joke is:
check your own
voice-mail message.

Just Try This ...
Call yourself and see
if you get the impression
that you are a first-class, creative person
who is obviously better than
the competition.
*Now record a better, more
creative message.*

Take Heart...
Most companies fail the
"be your own customer"
test miserably --
but at least now you know
what your customers
are up against.

18.5

THE LOYALTY MISSION: THE END OF SATISFACTION

- Your Mission Statement is wrong
- Your Mission Statement is wrong and sending the wrong message
- The Universal Mission Statement
- The End of Satisfaction is the Beginning of Loyalty
- The only perspective that matters

YOUR MISSION STATEMENT IS WRONG...

HINT: Is it in terms of the customer or the company?
BIGGER HINT: Who wrote it?
BIGGEST HINT: Who in your company uses it in the daily execution of their job? Do you?

Get Real...

• Who can recite your mission statement by heart?

• Who knows what your mission statement means?

• Who uses it in the daily performance of their job?

• Who is on the mission?

• Are you on the mission?

SO...

How can you revise your mission statement so that it's in terms of the customer, AND so that everyone executes it every time they face a customer -- including you!?

ANSWER...

Next two pages.

YOUR MISSION STATEMENT IS SENDING THE WRONG MESSAGE.

We're the best, we're the greatest, we're number one, we're the leader -- what a bunch of crap. Who wants to hear that? Number one what? Leader of what?

The problem with mission statements is that they are just that -- a statement -- not a statement with a purpose, not a statement in terms of the customer, not a statement people can understand, not a statement people can identify with and implement at each transaction.

They make a *statement* not a statement with an *identifiable purpose*. Something employees can remember and execute every time they're in front of a customer.

Here are the big 7.5 questions you may want to ask yourself about your existing mission statement.
1. Where would your company be without your customers?
2. Do you really think a customer cares about your mission statement written the way it is?
3. Why have a mission statement that the people who are most important to your company (the customer) could care less about?
4. Can anyone in your company (CEO included) recite your mission statement?
5. Does anyone in your company think about the mission statement when interacting with a customer?
6. Can anyone in your company identify with your mission statement?
7. Does anyone in your company live by your mission statement?
7.5 Did your advertising agency or marketing department write your mission statement in a vacuum (without input from employees and customers)?

If the only "yes" answer is number 7.5, you're in trouble -- and your competition is jumping for joy. Now that you're squirming, you might want to look at changing yours to reflect customer dedication in a way THE CUSTOMER gets it -- not how your ad agency writes it (major clue -- get your customers to help you write your mission statement, not a hired gun who couldn't care less).

18.5

The Loyalty Mission: The End of Satisfaction

Universal mission statement...

TREAT EVERY CUSTOMER

(client, patient, passenger, subscriber, guest, member)

IN SUCH A MEMORABLE WAY
THAT WHEN THE
TRANSACTION IS COMPLETE,
THE CUSTOMER
TELLS SOMEONE ELSE HOW

GREAT

IT WAS!

*What
does your
mission statement
say?*

*Once you realize
that "satisfaction" is
the lowest level of acceptable service,
you at once understand
the power of "loyalty."*

*How you achieve loyalty is a process,
not a single action.*

*Those who are able to achieve
loyalty from their customers for their
company and to themselves will be
the ones to get beyond success...
to fulfillment.*

I hope you do.

In the end,

the **only** perspective

that matters is

the customer's.

Epilogue

Thank you, angels!

Man thinks, God laughs is an old Jewish proverb.
And as I sit here thinking of what led me to this moment,
what circumstances created this opportunity, who helped me
get here, and how all this happened, I know there's a God
somewhere laughing until the tears are streaming down his face.
I just worked hard, and the right answers appeared as if by
magic. My ever present, extremely expensive
guardian angels handled the rest.

*Those angels here on earth
who have made significant contributions are:*

Thank you, Rod Smith

We had worked together on *The Sales Bible*. When I invited
Rod to help me finish editing this book, I thought I was 80%
done. I was wrong. He ripped, created, challenged, came up
with great ideas, and worked his brain off for 8 days to help
make this book what it is. Rod Smith is creative, funny, giving,
insightful, smart, and has a heart of gold. But the best part
about Rod Smith is that he is a person of character and ideals,
who doesn't just espouse them, he lives by them. That kind
of person is a privilege to know. I thank him for his
contribution, and I'm grateful for his friendship.

Thank you, gary hixson

I didn't understand hixson at first. I knew he had talent, but I
never pictured us working together. As I came to know him better,
his personality and character unfolded, and I began to see the
creative genius that he possessed. The cover and the interior
design of this book (among other things) are the thought and
creation of hixson. But the best part of his character is --
gary hixson is not just an angel to me -- he is an angel
to all he meets. What a gift.

Thank you, Ray Bard

I found Ray Bard on a referral from David Hahn at Planned Television Arts. The moment I talked to Ray I knew we had a deal. He was different from any other publisher I'd ever talked to. The first thing he did was go to the bookstore and BUY a copy of *The Sales Bible* (my first book) to see what kind of writer I was. (He liked it!) Then he flew to Dallas to meet me and watch me do a live seminar and negotiate this book deal face-to-face. Bard has character, honor, and integrity. He also knows the book business. What makes him rise above the rest is that he lives what he does, and he loves what he does.

Thank you, to the Buy|Gitomer team...
The Great Carrie Trueax
The Great Teresa Schumann

I am blessed and surrounded with the nicest people in the world. People who support me and help me every day. As I travel the world, EVERY person who has talked to anyone at our office ALWAYS goes out of their way to compliment me on how wonderful they are treated and how nice our staff is. I only hire eagles, happy people with great attitudes who are smart, funny, and overqualified. I thank everyone who has been here and look forward to the next one who flies in from the great beyond. Carrie Trueax came here via family intervention -- or should I say divine intervention. Since her arrival, she has excelled in every task -- she is now Queen of Faxes, Shipping & Inventory with more glory on the horizon. But the best blessing I received is Teresa Schumann. She came into the office and took charge in a way that no one has before. She has also taken charge of my heart. What a peaceful feeling that has been.

Thank you, customers

Over the past few years, more than 500 groups and companies have asked me to present my programs to more than 150,000 people. You have given me the opportunity to share what I have learned -- and you have taught me new things at the same time. Each presentation is a learning experience and a stepping stone. Each audience is joy and a pleasure. I thank you for the privilege. Each one of you.

Thank you, readers of the column

We receive over 1,000 responses a week to the "Sales Moves" column -- now in its seventh year. I love to read the notes from people who made a sale or saved a customer. They are inspiration for the next column. The "Sales Moves" column will continue weekly until I'm dead. I would also like to thank the weekly *Business Journals* and the people who publish and edit my column. They have had a significant positive impact on my career. Please subscribe to the *Business Journal* in your city.
Today.

Thank you, Glenn W. Turner

Between this book and the last, I got to meet and befriend the great Glenn W. Turner. During my 24th year, I listened to his tapes and watched "Challenge to America" hundreds of times, until my attitude changed from negative to positive -- where it has remained for the past 27 years. Meeting Glenn was a thrill, but getting to know him is the thrill of a lifetime.

Thank you, NSA

Last year (1997) at the National Speakers Association (NSA), I earned the Certified Speaking Professional (CSP) designation. It was a proud moment -- but the real pride is gleaned from the fact that I have met and learned from some of the finest, most sharing people in the world.

Thank you, friends and supporters

To my Charlotte friends and my friends in far away cities -- the people who believe in me, people who encourage me, people who are kind to me, people who challenge me, people who I laugh with and cry with, I say thank you, and wish that you could see my swollen heart from the pride of associating and spending time with the nicest people in the world.

Thank you, Erika, Stacey, Rebecca, Josh, Florrie, Max, and Lito

Max, my dad, still stands as the benchmark for my achievement, and Florrie, my mom, watches from heaven above to be sure my diction is correct. Parents get smarter as you get older. Josh, my brother, has been a constant inspiration for word frugality -- and I often listen to his Mount Madonna Choir CD -- it's music for the writer's spirit.

The kids, Erika, Stacey, and Rebecca, are growing up, getting married, getting pregnant, having children of their own, beautiful to look at, and a joy to be with and talk to. They are maturing into fine young women. I am proud of what they have become. They are the strongest silent inspiration, and the purest definition of love in the universe.

And Lito is still here to greet me when I come back. So are the newest additions to the litter: Bamboo and Sydney.

My father, my friend passed away April 13, 1998.

On his death bed I reminded him of visiting-day in 1960 when parents came to summer camp for the weekend to visit their children. The camp counselors played against the fathers. My dad came up to the plate and hit a ball out of the field of play and over the tennis courts. The counselors gave him an ovation. I was so proud. My dad was the best of all the other guys' dads.

And fathers want the same for their sons. To be proud of them. In one of our recent conversations he said, "Sonny boy, the old man's real proud of you." I just said, "thanks, pop," but inside I was as fulfilled as possible.

Like any 52 year relationship there were good times and bad. Like any good student I learned lessons from both. And in the end, I got a chance to tell him I love him and kiss him good-bye until the next time. I am sure there will be a next time.

And as for this time -- my dad was proud of me -- what else better can there be? What finer gift could you wish from your father?

Every day I either get on the airplane,
talk to an audience, type on my Macintosh,
make a sale, make a deal, or all of the above.
Life is full. And in full bloom.
I'm doing what I love to do, and I'm having
a blast at it every second. I learned something
new yesterday, today is a wonderful day,
and I can't wait for tomorrow.
All days are the same -- Holidays.

And I have you to thank for it.

My name is Jeffrey Gitomer.
I give value first,
I help other people,
I strive to be the best at what I love to do,
I establish long-term relationships with everyone,
and I have fun,
and I do that every day.

about the author
JEFFREY GITOMER, Chief Executive Salesman

Sales, Customer Service, and Personal Development Educator --
Seminar Leader -- Author -- Syndicated Columnist -- Dad --
Grand-pop

Gitomer's column... **Sales Moves**,
now in its tenth year of publication, appears in more than 85
business newspapers and is read weekly by more than 3,500,000
people.

Gitomer's first book... **The Sales Bible**,
now in its 14th printing, is acclaimed by The Dale Carnegie Sales
Training program, corporate trainers, corporate CEO's and salespeople across America. *The Sales Bible* has been translated into
Chinese and has sold more than 150,000 copies.

Gitomer's web-based training... **Trainone.com**,
provides weekly sales training over the Internet using streaming
video to salespeople around the world. A 15-20 minute in-depth
lesson each week to increase retention and boost sales.

Jeffrey Gitomer gives 100 *personalized, real-world* seminars, keynotes, runs annual sales meetings and customer service workshops
each year. His sales and customer service programs are developed
from 48 years (started when he was 7 years old) of on-the-street
selling. He has cold-called Fortune 500 presidents and made the
sale. In 1997, Jeffrey was awarded the designation of *Certified
Speaking Professional* (CSP) by The National Speakers Association.

Jeffrey grew up in New Jersey, but now lives in
Charlotte, NC -- *home of the Carolina Panthers.*

about
BUY|GITOMER

and the help you can get from Jeffrey Gitomer and his team of happy, intelligent, fun-to-deal-with people.

We specialize in one thing -- *helping You!*

Got a question?
Need a personalized workshop or seminar?
Have an annual meeting soon?
Want to make all your customers buy again?
Want more referrals?
Looking for more sales?
Driving to be number one?
Hate your competition and tired of competing?
Making the switch from satisfied customers...
to loyal customers?
Want a great book?
Listen to tapes in the car?
Searching for an answer?
Just want to talk?

Call us -- We can help!

Dynamic, inspirational, real-world, fun, funny, information-packed, take-to-the-bank, fatten-your-wallet seminars, keynotes, workshops, books, tapes, and videos on every aspect of sales and customer service.

BUY|GITOMER

310 Arlington Avenue, Loft 329
Charlotte, NC 28203
office 704.333.1112   fax 704.333.1011
e-mail salesman@gitomer.com

www.gitomer.com *and* www.trainone.com

Index

Every person in your
company should own this book.

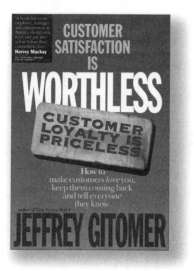

Visit your favorite bookstore

or

call 704.333.1112

or

fax 704.333.1011

or

e-mail jeffrey@gitomer.com

or

visit our Web sites

www.gitomer.com

and

www.trainone.com

(Quantity discounts are available.)

Loyal
is the most difficult
of the customer service
goals to achieve.

But once you have it,
you have something
your competition will
never have --

the next order.

On-the-Job
instruction and
inspiration

24 action cards excerpted from the book
Customer Satisfaction is Worthless
Customer Loyalty is Priceless
BY JEFFREY GITOMER

BUY|GITOMER
310 Arlington Avenue, Loft 329
Charlotte, NC 28203
704.333.1112 office
704.333.1011 fax
e-mail salesman@gitomer.com

www.gitomer.com *and* **www.trainone.com**

The Big Secret...

Quality performance (and quality service) starts with a positive attitude!

A gentle reminder...

Word-of-Mouth advertising is the most powerful form of advertising in the world.

Here's how it works...

The customer is always wrong...
and you're just about as perfect!

It's not about right or wrong — it's how you *react to* and handle the problem.

The best way to get loyalty is to give loyalty.

JEFFREY GITOMER

Get Real...

How do YOU like dealing with a customer service person that's indifferent or has a lousy attitude? You'd better create and deliver positive first words before your competition catches on.

Just Try This...

Read about positive attitude for 15 minutes each morning for thirty days. Then write down the best quote of the day. A sentence or two that inspired you. Take it into work -- enter it in your computer -- make it fancy -- print it out, and put copies on everyone else's computer screen.

Customers talk...

to their associates, friends, and neighbors.

Here is the number of people they will talk to based upon how well you handle their complaint.

3 if you do a good job
10 if you do a great job
25 if you do a bad job
50 if you get into an argument

and -- if the argument develops into a fight, and your lawyers get involved, you will be on the 6:00pm local news.

How are your customers talking about you?

Could the problem be YOU?

THE THREE-OPTION OPPORTUNITY

The most powerful Customer Service lesson in the world

Customers don't make up stories about your business -- it is you who create them. The customer simply retells them. How the story is told, and what the content is, is up to you.

The story will be re-told to fellow workers, business associates, family members and/or friends, about your customer's experiences with you. This presents a three-option opportunity:

1. To say something good about you and your business.
2. To say nothing about you and your business.
3. To say something bad about you and your business.

Train on these before you even dream of opening your policy book.

Principle 1. Your customer is your paycheck. JUST TRY THIS: The more you work for the customer's success, the more you will earn.

Principle 2. Your attitude (the way you dedicate yourself to the way you think) determines the degree of excellence of service you will perform. JUST TRY THIS: Read about positive attitude for 15 minutes each morning. Create and deliver positive first words. Do whatever it takes to maintain your positive attitude.

Principle 3. Customers call, contact, or visit for one reason -- they need HELP! JUST TRY THIS: Know why your customers call, and the BEST way to respond to each need.

Principle 12.5 The customer's PERCEPTION of good or bad service is the measure of your success or failure.

JUST TRY THIS: Master the elements of service that customers consider most important. How do you find out what they are? You ask them (duh). How do you master them? You work at being your best every day.

Principle 7. When you're done speaking with a customer or the transaction is over, that's when they START talking. JUST TRY THIS: Start positive, end positive, and put positive in the middle.

Principle 8. Word-of-mouth advertising is 50 times more powerful than advertising. JUST TRY THIS: Write down things that help customers, speak at trade shows and business functions -- get in front of people who can say "yes" to you, and deliver value first.

Principle 9. Your friendliness and willingness to help is in direct proportion to your success. JUST TRY THIS: Start friendly, end friendly, and put friendly in the middle.

continued

Treat *every* customer as though they were your favorite celebrity, hero, friend, neighbor, or your **grandma.**

How else might you think of your customer?

Principle 10. Company policy is written in terms of the company, not the customer. It tells you what you can't do for a customer -- not what you can do. It tells you what you can't do for a customer situation, start out by saying -- "in order to be fair to everyone..."

Principle 11. Service is a feeling. You know what it is when you get it -- so give back the same thing -- or more. JUST TRY THIS: Remember how you felt the last time you got great service? Give that to your customers. *Every day.*

Principle 12. The secret to customer service success of is -- start with YES. JUST TRY THIS: Start your response with -- "The best way to get that done is..." or "The easiest (fastest) way to do that is..." MAJOR SERVICE SUCCESS CLUE: Institute a policy that states you must have a manager's approval before you can tell a customer "no." *continued*

Every time a customer calls
or you call a customer --
you have an opportunity
and a choice.

What choice are you making?

GetReal...

JustTryThis...

Are you creating frequent, lasting, memorable impressions?

Name one.

Principle 4. The value of a customer is 20 times his annual sales volume. JUST TRY THIS: Every customer contact is an opportunity to earn the next sale. Be your best on every customer interaction.

Principle 5. A customer ready to repeat his purchase is a powerful business advantage. JUST TRY THIS: Substitute relationship-building strategies for sales techniques. Stay in front of your customer in times of "non-sale" as much as you do in times of "sale."

Principle 6. Customer satisfaction is worthless. Satisfaction is no longer the acceptable standard of customer service. JUST TRY THIS: Understand what makes you loyal, and employ those actions toward your customers.

continued

HERE ARE 7.5 ADVANTAGES OF GREAT SERVICE...

1. It's free. *Great service costs little or nothing -- but it's worth a fortune.*
2. It builds goodwill. *Consistent service creates and builds reputation.*
3. It builds customer loyalty. *People will actually look forward to the next time they'll do business with you. They're happy to do business with you.*
4. It creates memorable experiences that will be retold time after time. *Stories create the basis of word-of-mouth advertising.*
5. It makes your customers salesperson for your business. *And they are one thousand times more effective than any employed salesperson on your team.*
6. It leads to referred business. *People are guided and influenced by the success, satisfaction, and happiness of others.*
7. It makes it harder (impossible) for competitors to steal away customers -- even at a lower price. *"Loyalty through extra-ordinary service" is a powerful -- yet overlooked -- motto in business today.*
7.5 It creates a clear distinction between two companies engaged in the same business. *Yours and your biggest competitor.*

The secret words are...
Oh, that's horrible!

(said with extreme empathy and feeling)

These secret words not only stop the customer from complaining, but it lets you begin to get to resolve and solution. The customer does not want to hear a bunch of your lame excuses about why it didn't work, or didn't happen. The customer only wants to know you CARE, and what you're going to do about it -- NOW!

When you say "Oh, that's horrible," it immediately lets the customer know you're on their side. The customer is expecting you to provoke an argument. When you say, "Oh, that's horrible" -- the argument's over. Try it -- the results are amazing.

Jeffrey Gitomer's *Personal Touch Method*
How to handle an angry customer.

Here are 14.5 steps to taking responsibility when dealing with unhappy or dissatisfied customers:

1. Tell them you understand how they feel.
2. Empathize with them. Tell them a similar thing happened to you. *Comfort them.*
3. Listen all the way out. Don't interrupt. Ask questions to understand their problem better, and to find out what it will take to help them.
4. Agree with them if at all possible. *(Never argue or get angry.)*
5. Take notes and confirm back that everything has been covered.
6. Be an ambassador for your company. Tell the customer you will personally handle it.
7. Don't blame others or look for a scapegoat. Take responsibility for correcting it.
   continued

It's all in the first few words...

The way the customer hears your words will determine his or her thoughts of being satisfied or helped. Here are the Prime Starting Phrases that will get the ball rolling in the right direction.

Say it the way you would want to hear it. Just change a few pronouns or ask a question instead of making a negative statement.

The secret is in the first few words.

Get a Complaint?

When you take the call or complaint -- even though it may not be your job, or you may not be the person who deals with the complaint, you are the person who is responsible to see that it gets done or is handled.

Your job is to communicate it and follow up afterward.

If you field the call, it's up to you to be responsible, *even though you are not the person who may take the action.*

Three more secret words are...
You're in luck!

I tried to make an immediate appointment at a recording studio -- The woman on the other end of the phone said -- "You can't do it until Friday. We're booked solid until then. We can't take you."

Couldn't she have just as easily said...
"Jeffrey, you're in luck! -- I've got a spot open on Friday."

Same message -- different language.
Much different feeling.
How do you say it?
Start with "You're in luck!"

Jeffrey Gitomer's Personal Touch Method
How to handle an angry customer.

8. Don't pass the buck. *"It's not my job..." is never acceptable to the customer.*
9. Respond immediately. *The customer wants it now.*
10. Find some common ground other than the problem.
11. Use humor if possible. *Making people laugh puts them at ease.* (*Try to establish some rapport.*)
12. Figure out, communicate, and agree upon a solution or resolution. Confirm it (in writing if necessary). *Tell them what you plan to do... and DO IT!*
13. Make a follow-up call after the situation is resolved.
14. Get a favorable letter if you can.
14.5 Ask yourself: *"What have I learned, and what can I do to prevent this situation from happening again? Do I need to make changes?"*

JustTryThese...

After the customer makes a request, or asks a question, or gripes -- before you answer the request or question, say things like...

Great!
No problem!
That's my favorite problem!
I think we can solve...
I'm sure there's a way...
I think I can help!
Yes!
Cool!
Can do!
Consider it done!

or, use the "start with yes" phrases: The best way to handle that is...The fastest way to get that done is...

GetReal...

If you own the problem, you own the customer.
If you lose the problem, you lose the customer.

It's just that simple.

PRINCIPLE 2

YOUR ATTITUDE

(the way you dedicate yourself to the way you think)

DETERMINES THE DEGREE OF EXCELLENCE OF SERVICE YOU PERFORM.

PRINCIPLE 11

SERVICE IS A FEELING.

You know what it is when you get it – so give back the same thing – or more. The simple secret is – don't give any feeling to others that you wouldn't want to feel. You know when you're doing a good job, you can feel it. You also know when you're doing your BEST. It's an inside feeling of YES!

It's only possible to get that feeling when you're concentrating on building a better self. A better YOU. It takes a daily self-discipline and re-dedication to your positive attitude every morning. It's study, it's reading. It's spending quality time building the character of the most important person in the world. But it's worth it – I promise.

How do you feel on the inside after each customer interaction?

The Challenge for the 21st century is not just serving customers…

- It's understanding customers.
- It's being prepared to serve customers.
- It's helping an angry customer *immediately*.
- It's asking customers for information.
- It's listening to customers.
- It's being responsible for your actions when a customer calls.
- It's living up to your commitments.
- It's being memorable.
- It's surprising customers.
- It's striving to keep customers for life.
- It's getting unsolicited referrals from customers…*regularly!*

PRINCIPLE 9

YOUR FRIENDLINESS AND WILLINGNESS TO HELP IS IN DIRECT PROPORTION TO YOUR SUCCESS.

POSITIVE ATTITUDE

POSITIVE ATTITUDE is the foundation of your life -- and the determining factor of your ability to serve. Your positive attitude has the best possibility of creating positive customer perception of your entire company. How positive (enthusiastic and friendly) are the first words spoken to your customer?

How consistent is your positive attitude?
Do you spend 15 minutes a morning reading positive information to get your day going?

GetReal...
Service is a feeling and you know what it is -- whether it's good or bad. If you can't remember what "bad" feels like, call the DMV, IRS, or Social Security. That's bad. Then call L.L. Bean -- that's good. See the difference?

JustTryThis...
Remember how you felt the last time you got great service? Target five great customers and create a simple plan to make them feel GREAT.

Goal: Try to get one unsolicited letter of praise for the way you made someone feel.

What else would customers like?

VALUE "I want to know that what I'm buying is at a fair price, and will be supported throughout the length of my ownership."

COMMUNICATION "Let me know what I need to know, when I need to know it."

ATTITUDE "Happy, eager, willing...prepared to meet my needs."

RELIABILITY "Consistent...be there when I need you."

TANGIBILITY "Quality of product and performance...professional image."

ASSURANCE "Deliver when you promised...total product knowledge."

EMPATHY "Understand me and my needs. Give me your commitment."

EXCEPTIONAL SERVICE "I vote with my money, and an election is held every time I want to re-order or tell a friend."

All things being equal, people want to do business with friends. All things being not quite equal, people want to do business with friends. The best way to get to be friends is to be friendly.

How friendly are you?
When a customer calls with a problem, do you try to get rid of it, or are you the person who solves it?

It is important to be aware of some practical realities when trying to accomplish the task of (recovery) satisfying the angry customer. They are:

- The customer knows exactly how they want it, or exactly what they want, but may be a lousy communicator and not tell you completely, or tell you in a way that is difficult to understand. **If the customer cannot state his complaint in a clear and concise manner, it's up to you to help him do so.**
- Remember, you're the customer elsewhere. *Think about the level of service you expect when you're the customer.*
- Every customer thinks he's the only one you've got... Treat him that way. *Make the customer feel important.*
- The customer is human and has problems, just like you do.
- The customer expects service at the flip of a switch.
- It all boils down to you.
- The customer's perception is reality.
- How big a deal is it to try to give the customer what he wants?

ARE YOU USING THE WOW! FACTOR?

One of the most powerful aspects of sales: being different.

What is WOW!?... WOW! is great service!

WOW! separates the EXTRAordinary from the ordinary.

WOW! separates the strong from the weak.

WOW! separates the sincere from the insincere.

WOW! separates the pro's from the con's.

WOW! separates the yes's from the no's.

WOW! is the full measure of your personal power and the way you use it.

Are you WOW! Is WOW! a factor in your serving process? How do you WOW! the customer?

START WITH... YES!

The secret to successful customer service is...

Instead of giving the customer a bunch of lame excuses or reasons you can't do what they want – start your response with – "The best way to get that done is..." or "The easiest (fastest) way to do that is..." Give solutions, not excuses. That's what customers want.

"The best way to handle that is..."

"The fastest way to get that done is..."

"The easiest way to get that is..."

Do you ALWAYS start with yes? Do you ALWAYS offer the solution?

WANT A DAILY REPORT CARD?

WATCH, LOOK & LISTEN!

Watch for smiles – when you get them, you're on the right path!

Look for unsolicited letters of thanks and praise – when you get them, you're on the right path!

Listen for "thanks" – when you hear it, you're on the right path! and...

Listen for "WOW!" – when you hear WOW! you're on *THE* path!

GetReal...

RECOVERY IS POWERFUL.

When you satisfy an unhappy or dissatisfied customer, and you can get them to write you a letter telling you they're happy and satisfied now, I'd say you have a solid shot at a long-term relationship.

If the problem is left unresolved... the customer will surely find your competition.

BE **WOW!** YOURSELF --

You must be positive, enthusiastic, focused, polished, and convinced. You must be outstanding enough to be memorable.

- Focus on your customer.
- Put your passion in your actions.
- Don't ever let them see you sweat.
- Let them feel your belief in yourself, your product, and your company.
- Never quit.
- Have your dreams ever present in your mind.

In service it all boils down to the one word customers want to hear...yes!

Get there with **WOW!**, and the sky is your limit!

GetReal...

Isn't YES what you want to hear when you're the customer?

JustTryThis...

Post the three responses above by your telephone (next to the pictures of your children eating). For the next week, start every response with -- "The best way to get that done is..." or "The easiest (fastest) way to do that is..." Watch the change in the way customers respond to you.

Here are two success strategies to ensure that you are realistic about your performance and prepared to become better every day.

1. Record yourself once a week. Listen to how you sound. Listen to your tone of voice. Listen to how you respond. Listen to how you take responsibility. Is that who you would want service from? Listening to yourself is painful and powerful.

2. Take some kind of training every day. If you want to be great, you must learn how to get there. (Managers: If you want great people, it's your responsibility to train them to be great.)

IT'S OUR POLICY...
TO PISS OFF EVERYONE!

Policy is written to tell you what you can't do -- and it's the single most annoying word to a customer besides "no" (and one is really just another word for the other).

JustTryThis...The next time you have to refer to the rules of the company, use this phrase instead of the word "policy":

"In order to be fair to everyone..."

has a ring of humanity about it, and it almost sounds positive.

CAUTION: *This is not a panacea -- it will not satisfy everyone every time -- but it's a better alternative than the one you're using now.*

A Positive Attitude...
(the way you dedicate yourself to the way you think and act)

is your ability to think, listen, speak, and react in a purely positive way.

To see the good in things...not the bad; to see how to make bad things good.

To see the opportunity when an obstacle faces you.

To see things from the what is right side...not the what is wrong side.

To treat others the way you want to be treated.

To encourage others when they need support.

To forgive others who have hurt or offended you.

To never let the negative things of the world effect/affect you for more than 5 minutes.

To (almost) never have a bad day.

To have something nice or humorous to say.

To be internally happy.

To work at maintaining your attitude every day.

When you can add to the end of each sentence..."all the time" you've got a positive attitude.

A personal challenge
from the Great Jim Rohn:

"Formal education will earn you a living.

Self-education will earn you a fortune.

You determine how much of a fortune you will earn by how much self-education you decide to get."

WOW!

JustTryThis...

Here's a way to ensure you understand who the customer is. Every time you lose a customer, and he stops doing business with your company -- the net result from the loss of revenue is...

Your kids eat less!

Go home tonight and, at the dinner table, take a picture of your children -- *eating*.

Put copies of the picture on the dashboard of your car, your telephone, and your computer screen.

If you don't have any children, go home to your parents' house and let them take a picture of YOU eating -- same thing.

Get Real...

Do you like it when someone gives you "the policy"? Kind of sounds like "the finger." Wouldn't you rather hear "In order to be fair to everyone..."?

Your customers didn't call to get a lesson in your policy, they called to get help -- *and if you don't give it to them, they'll call someplace else.*

Angry customers...

- they may have a health problem
- they may have a spouse problem
- they may have a money problem

They may be taking that out on you.

JustTryThis...

Take it seriously -- not personally.

Shouldn't it really be called **"Customer Helping"** rather than customer service?

AND

wouldn't you deliver better service if you thought of it that way?

Put **"Grandma"** at the end of everything you say.

How would this sound?

- Sorry we're closed, Grandma.
- Next Grandma.
- What is this in reference to, Grandma?
- It's our policy, Grandma.

Get it?

Get Real...

If you wouldn't say it to your grandma, why would you say it to your customer?